INTERESTING STORIES FOR CURIOUS MINDS

A BOOK OF FASCINATING TRIVIA, SHORT STORIES & FUN FACTS FOR ADULTS

MARGARET LASHLEY

WHAT READERS ARE SAYING

"A delightful book chock full of fun and fascinating trivia for those of us who want to enjoy the weird and wonderful things our world has to offer." — The Book Lush

INTRODUCTION

Hello!

Welcome to Volume One of *Interesting Stories for Curious Minds*. I'm glad you're here!

If history teaches us anything, it's that the truth is often stranger (and *way* more intriguing) than fiction. This book is proof positive that the world is full of fascinating people, weird places, and oddly hilarious things.

Where do I get my stories? As a professional advertising writer and mystery novelist, I'm always on the search for interesting ways to amuse and surprise my readers. In other words, I do a lot of research.

I work hard to uncover the craziest things on the planet, so you don't have to!

Whether you're a trivia maven or simply enjoy learning new things that aren't common knowledge, you'll find plenty to keep you entertained. No dry lists of boring facts. And nothing truly gruesome or explicit. Just light-hearted reading perfect for curious adults, teens, and seniors.

So sit back and enjoy—and prepare to learn and laugh.

Happy reading, and all my best,

Margaret Lashley

P.S. To get a FREE bonus story, go to: https://dl.bookfun nel.com/i7y7o1dvnp

CHAPTER 1
A BLOWOUT PERFORMANCE

AT ONE TIME, the country of France led the world in culture, raising the bar around the globe for wine, fashion, and haute cuisine. But few people know the French also gave rise to a rather odd "musical" entertainer named Joseph Pujol.

Pujol was a farteur—a professional farter.

Born in 1857, he discovered his unusual talents as a child. While swimming in the sea one day, he ducked under water and held his breath. Suddenly, he felt an icy cold penetrate his sphincter. Frightened, he ran ashore and was stupefied to find water pouring from his anus.

Had Pujol been a woman, modesty might have put an end to this story. But Pujol was a guy, and when he joined the army, he couldn't help but brag to his fellow soldiers about his "special ability." For their amusement, he would sit in a pan of water, sucking it up into his colon, then stand and "project" the water from his rear-end for distances up to several yards.

At some point, in a eureka moment, Pujol discovered he could also suck up air. And the rest, as they say, is history.

A baker by trade, Pujol began entertaining his regular customers by imitating musical instruments, then claiming he was playing them behind the counter. After "fine-tuning" his talents, Pujol decided he would be amiss not to share his unique gift with the world.

But first, he needed a stage name. What was the fledgling fartiste to call himself? Pujol settled on Le Pétomane, a combination of *péter* (French for "to fart") and *mane* (French for "maniac"). In other words, Pujol called himself, The Fartomaniac.

His fartiste act debuted in 1887 in Marseilles, where it was so well received that Pujol moved to Paris and became a star attraction at the Moulin Rouge.

Some highlights of his act included imitating the sounds of cannon fire and thunderstorms. By attaching a rubber hose to an ocarina (a vessel flute the size and shape of a golf-club-head) and inserting the other end ... well, you know where ... Pujol "played" such hits as *O Sole Mio*, and, of course, the French national anthem, *La Marseillaise*.

At the height of his fame, Pujol attracted audience members including Edward, Prince of Wales, King Leopold II of Belgium, and, interestingly, Sigmund Freud. (I guess sometimes a fart is *not* just a fart.)

When WWI broke out, Pujol left the stage and returned to baking. He died in 1945 at the age of 88. But his artful and airy legacy lives on in popular culture.

For instance, in the 1974 movie *Blazing Saddles*, Mel Brooks appears in multiple roles, including a dim-witted governor named William J. Le Petomane, a tongue-in-cheek allusion to the possibility he was full of hot air.

Pujol's Le Pétomane character also inspired several musicals, including *The Fartiste*, awarded Best Musical at the 2006

New York International Fringe Festival, and *A Passing Wind*, which premiered at the 2011 Philadelphia International Festival of the Arts.

(Seriously, what passes for entertainment never ceases to amaze me.)

It's a common misconception that Pujol actually passed gas as part of his stage performance. In truth, he was a fake-farter, allegedly able to "inhale" air into his rectum, then control the release through deft manipulation of his sphincter muscles. While this seems like a rather wild claim, it was corroborated by his fellow soldiers who witnessed the farteur's early—and apparently more explicit—demonstrations.

Fun Fact: Unlike many cultures that cringe with embarrassment over passing gas in public, the Germans aren't quite as shy about it. In fact, they even use funny names for some of their more flatulence-inducing dishes. A popular onion-filled pastry is called Trumpet Pie. And a regional cheese dish from Frankfurt is named Handkäse mit Musik. (Handmade cheese with "music.")

CHAPTER 2
SLUGGING IT OUT OVER RODENT STEW

THE LATE, great Queen Elizabeth of England was the epitome of poise and grace. Before her death in 2022, she reigned for 70 years and 214 days—the longest verified reign of any female monarch in history.

Like any job, the position had its perks and its quirks. So did Her Majesty. Especially when it came to food.

For instance, Queen Elizabeth avoided garlic, mainly due to its breath-defying stench. She also avoided starchy side dishes like pasta and potatoes. And, like the privileged person she was, she insisted that the sharp, crusty corners of sandwiches be removed before served with her daily tea.

But while traveling outside her domain, the Queen proved to be a much less persnickety eater. As the royal representative of the United Kingdom, she was often requested to sample local cuisine. Out of respect for the host country's culture, she rarely failed to oblige.

In 1986, while touring China, the Queen was served a three-inch-long slimy sea slug. Well within her rights to politely decline, she did no such thing. Instead, the Queen elegantly grasped her ivory chopsticks and took a bite, then declared it delicious. (She later described the taste as something like shrimp, but milder, saying the slug "tasted of not much.")

Apparently, the Queen was as eloquent as she was elegant. Perhaps she'd honed her curious epicurean talents the year before, while on a tour of Central America. In 1985, her entourage stopped in the newly independent country of Belize, where she was served a local delicacy of gibnut stew.

The gibnut, which can grow up to 30 inches in length and weigh up to 31 pounds, is considered "bush meat." It's one of the few native animals locals hunted in Belize's rainforests. Oh, and did I mention that the gibut is a member of the rodent family?

Yes. The gibnut is a very large cousin of the common rat. In other words, the Belizeans served the Queen rat stew.

Unfazed by the genetic lineage of her entrée, Her Majesty declared gibnut tasted "like rabbit" and heartily ate her stew alongside her hosts.

Today, because of this, Belizeans often refer to the gibnut as the "royal rat." Even now, restaurants still advertise the dish on their menus, referring to it as "the rat eaten by Her Majesty Queen Elizabeth" in an effort to drum up business.

Even so, I think I'd pass. How about you?

Fun Fact: Besides consuming strange animals, the Queen of England was often gifted *live* ones. While most were horses and livestock of varying breeds, many were most definitely not. What's a Queen to do with an emu? Often, the more exotic specimens found homes in the ZSL London Zoo.

Some of the Queen's most unusual animal gifts included:

- A pair of pygmy hippopotami from the President of Liberia
- A young Nile crocodile from the People of Berending on the Gambia River
- One sloth and two black jaguars from the Prefect of Brazilia
- An African forest elephant from the President of Cameroon
- Two Aldabra giant tortoises from the Government and People of the Seychelles
- Four bare-eyed cockatoos, two wallabies, and a dwarf cassowary from Taronga Zoo in Australia

CHAPTER 3
FAST FOOD GOES THE DISTANCE

"NEITHER SNOW nor rain nor heat nor gloom of night stays these couriers from the swift completion of their appointed rounds." While this popular phrase is often attributed to the US Postal Service, they don't claim it as their official motto.

Maybe it should go to fast-food delivery workers, instead.

In 1998, Japanese TV star Eiji Bando got on the phone and ordered a pie from Jerusalem 2, a kosher pizzeria across the ocean in New York City. Impressed with his customer's loyalty, the restaurant owner, Eddie Fishbaum, delivered the pizza in person. The 7,000 mile trip to Osaka, Japan cost about a buck a mile to complete. Who picked up the $7,000 check? That fact has been lost to history.

But we're just getting started in our long-distance love affair with fast food. In 2004, Domino's employee Lucy Clough carried a vegetarian "Supreme" pizza all the way from London, England to Melbourne, Australia. That's a distance of over 10,000 miles!

While traveling in Sydney, Australia in 2001, British hiker Rachel Kerr got a hankering for a curry. But not just any curry would do. It had to be the curry from Rupali, an Indian restaurant in Newcastle England. Not keen to miss a sale, the owner obliged, and made arrangements for Rachel's special order to be transported nearly 11,000 miles.

That same year, Cornè Krige, the then captain of the South African Fedsure Stormers rugby team, ordered a pie from Butlers Pizza. The only problem was, like Rachel, he also was in Sydney, Australia. But the 7,000 mile distance didn't stop employee Bernard Jordaan from hopping on a plane and hand-delivering the pizza to Krige's hotel room.

The longest curry delivery was ordered by UK citizens James Crisp and Jon Wise. They were dying to have a vegetable biryani and pilau rice from The Raj Mahal Restaurant in Christchurch, New Zealand. The food was dutifully delivered on February 29, 2008, to the Daily Sport offices in Manchester, UK. That was an impressive 11,701 miles, as the crow flies.

Those were some pretty impressive deliveries. But one tops them all. It was completed by FoodPanda, a major food delivery service popular in Asia. In 2022, a woman from Singapore named Maanasa Gopal crossed four continents and traversed 18,641 miles to deliver food to customers in Antarctica. Documenting her trip on Instagram, Gopal traveled from Singapore to Hamburg, Germany, then to Buenos Aires, Argentina before finally boarding a flight to Antarctica from Ushuaia.

Fun Fact: If you plan to order a pizza for your Martian football party held on the Red Planet, it would be best to call ahead. Traveling at a speed of 24,600 mph, the 300 million-mile trip would take Planetary Express Delivery (I just made that up) about seven months to get there. Don't forget to tip the astronaut!

CHAPTER 4
SUPPORT YOUR LOCAL ARTISTS—OR ELSE!

In 1907, a young, peace-loving vegetarian applied to the Academy of Fine Arts Vienna. He was rejected. He tried again the next year, and was again turned down. His hopes of becoming a professional artist dashed, he turned to another profession. Politics. Here, he would finally find the recognition he sought—and become directly responsible for the deaths of 50 million people.

After failing to gain entry to art school, the struggling artist spent time among artsy cafes in Vienna, hoping one of the master artists would take him in and teach him. No such luck. He even tried to make a living drawing postcards, but again met with failure.

Unable to find meaning or purpose for his life, he wandered the streets with the other poor, disillusioned citizens. There, he was repeatedly exposed to the anti-Semitic rhetoric of King Franz Josef I—namely that Jews were hoarding all of Austria's wealth, thus causing their economic woes.

Abject poverty, coupled with absolute rejection by the

upper crust of Vienna's art movement, unintentionally fostered the simmering hatred that would lead this would-be artist to become the dictator known as Adolf Hitler.

In his youth, Hitler was a prolific painter. In his book, *Mein Kampf* (My Struggle), he wrote that he produced two or three works a day. Over his lifespan, estimates of his total portfolio range from 300 to over 2,000 paintings.

But was Hitler any good as an artist? Well, as they say, beauty is in the eye of the beholder. Here's what a few critics had to say:

American journalist John Gunter reviewed the paintings Hitler submitted to the Vienna art academy and wrote, "They are prosaic, utterly devoid of rhythm, color, feeling, or spiritual imagination. They are architect's sketches: painful and precise craftsmanship, nothing more. No wonder the Vienna professors told him to go to an architectural school and give up pure art as hopeless."

Hauntingly, in 2002 a modern art critic was asked to review some of Hitler's paintings, unaware of who the artist was. The critic's opinion was that they were quite good, but that the different style in which he drew human figures represented *a profound disinterest in people.* (Spooky.)

Ironically, after the war, Hitler's paintings sold for up to $50,000 dollars apiece. Quite a stack of Deutschmarks for the time period. More recently, in 2014 one of his watercolors sold for $161,000. And a batch of 14 paintings sold in 2015 for $450,000.

Today, one of the most extensive private collections of Hitler's artwork is housed in Natick, Massachusetts at the International Museum of World War II.

But what if Hitler hadn't been rejected by the Vienna art school?

As published in the *British War Blue Book*, in August 1939, right before the outbreak of WWII, Hitler told British Ambassador Nevile Henderson that, "I am an artist and not a politician. Once the Polish question is settled, I want to end my life as an artist."

Wow. Food for thought next time you cross paths with any starving artists. You just might consider throwing them a bone. Or perhaps some tofu …

Fun Facts: Hitler was Austrian, not German. He refused to eat meat or broth, calling it "corpse tea." He designed the beloved Volkswagen Beetle. And, ironically, one of his paintings featured, "Mother Mary and the Holy Child Jesus Christ." Makes me wonder, what would Jesus do?

CHAPTER 5
LOST IN TRANSLATION

AFTER DEFEATING GERMANY IN WWII, allies divided the country into American, British, French and Soviet zones of occupation. Germany's capital city, Berlin, technically fell into the Soviet quadrant. But it was also divided, with the Soviets taking the eastern part.

In 1961, to avoid massive defections out of East Berlin, the Soviet Union built the infamous Berlin Wall, cutting off the communist east side from the non-communist west side.

Nearly two years after the wall's construction, during the middle of the Cold War, U.S. President John F. Kennedy visited West Berlin and delivered one of the most famous anti-communist speeches of all time.

Designed to be a morale booster for the citizens of West Berlin, Kennedy drew inspiration for his speech from Roman times, saying:

"Two thousand years ago, the proudest boast was *civis romanus sum*. (I am a Roman citizen.) Today, in the world of freedom, the proudest boast is, 'Ich bin ein Berliner!'"

The 120,000 Germans who'd gathered for the speech

cheered! Kennedy continued, "All free men, wherever they may live, are citizens of Berlin, and therefore, as a free man, I take pride in the words, ich bin ein Berliner!"

According to some, the second time Kennedy said the phrase, his Boston accent and/or perhaps a misreading of his phonetic notes (Ish bin ein Bearleener) affected his pronunciation and it sounded more like, "I am a jelly donut."

Why? Because in Germany, a Berliner is a citizen of Berlin, and a Berliner is also a jelly-filled donut. (Bear-LIN-er, Bear-LEEN-er. Po-TAY-to, Po-TAT-o.)

In his speech, Kennedy failed to mention what kind of jelly he contained. My guess would be raspberries…

Fun Fact: Kennedy performed his famous speech on the steps of the Rathaus Shöneberg. The fact that Rathaus (rat house) means Town Hall in German is yet another amusing factoid to chew on.

CHAPTER 6
THE FALL OF THE SOVIET PIZZA

WHATEVER HAPPENED TO PEACE, love and Perestroika?

During the late 1980s, the newly appointed General Secretary of the Communist Party, Mickhail Gorbachev, implemented some pretty mind-blowing changes for the Soviet Union. Namely, Perestroika (restructuring) and Glasnost (openness).

The idea was to try and develop new thinking that would eradicate a decade of poor living conditions, shortages, declining production, and economic stagnation in the USSR. Unfortunately, his ideas went over with his comrades like a lead babushka. In fact, Gorbachev became so disliked he had to hire actors to sing his praises.

So he turned to Pizza Hut for help.

Actually, he turned to the free-market economic model. Pizza Hut just happened to get their first. They opened their initial store in Moscow in 1990, even beating McDonald's to the capitalist punch! And in an even bolder move, Pizza Hut asked Gorbachev himself to star in their commercials.

Needless to say, after the collapse of the Soviet Union,

Gorbachev's pension plan had plummeted like a Scud missile. Even so, it took Pizza Hut a year of negotiations to get Gorbachev to do it.

The spot, created by BBDO ad agency, was filmed in Moscow in late 1997. In it, Gorbachev walks through the snow-lined streets with his granddaughter. They enter a Pizza Hut and are noticed by other patrons, who begin to bicker about the politician.

One man argues, "Because of him we have economic confusion."

His son rebuts, "Because of him, we have opportunity."

Then the man's wife says, "Because of him we have many things...like Pizza Hut."

The ad aired in 1998, but, ironically, was never seen in Russia. Gorbachev got a cool million bucks for the role.

What did Gorbachev do with the money? You can safely bet he didn't blow it all on personal pan pizzas. In fact, he refused to eat the pizza in the commercial, employing his granddaughter to do the deed. It's been reported that Gorbachev used the money to fund various research projects he was working on at the time.

Fun Fact: In 2007, the need for cash again led Gorbachev to mug for a manufacturer. This time, it was an ad for Louis Vuitton. In it, Gorbachev sits in the back seat of a car sporting the designer's high-end threads. In the background, the tattered remains of the Berlin Wall are clearly visible through the side window.

Ouch.

CHAPTER 7
STICKING IT TO THE MAN

STICK INSECTS, also known as walking sticks, are a true testament to Charles Darwin's theory of how species can adapt over time to better survive in their environments.

Darwin himself actually owned a walking stick—but not of the insect variety. He carried a white cane made of whalebone and ivory. It featured a carved skull on the top grip, complete with two piercing green eyes made of glass. He named it Morituri. But that's another story…

Darwin's most quotable saying is, "It is not the strongest of the species that survives, nor the most intelligent that survives. It is the one that is most adaptable to change."

Let me tell you, walking sticks are so adaptable, they could beat Rocky Balboa in the ring with one leg tied behind their backs. Not just because they can grow a new leg if Rocky rips one off, but because chances are highly likely Rocky would never see them coming in the first place.

Members of the *Phasmatodea* order, this bizarre family of insects has evolved over the eons to blend in so well with the plants they hang around on that they're virtually invisible to the untrained eye.

Typically brown, green, or black, they have thin, stick-shaped bodies that perfectly meld with plants' woody stems. Some species go the extra mile to add lichen-like blotches to their exoskeletons. Others even *act* like twigs, rocking their bodies back and forth along with the breeze, mimicking the movement of the plants they're perched upon.

But perhaps one of the most fascinating things about stick insects is their ability to reproduce parthenogenetically. (Say that three times fast.) What this means is, unfertilized females can still produce eggs that with hatch—but they will all be females. (If a male fertilizes an egg, it has a 50% chance of becoming a male.)

In captivity, a female stick insect can produce hundreds of all-female progeny without ever having mated. In fact, there are some species for which scientists have been unable to find any males. (Not even on MatchStick dot com.)

While stick insects aren't venomous, they aren't defense-less, either. When threatened, some species will barf out a nasty substance, putting a bad taste in the mouth of whoever's trying to eat them. Others reflex bleed, causing a foul-smelling hemolymph substance to ooze from their joints. Some can even direct a chemical spray similar to tear gas at their attackers. A few species can change color like a chameleon in order to blend even better into the background.

If all those cool tactics fail, there's always the old play-dead ruse. Here, the outmatched walking stick lets go of its grip and does a dead drop to the ground and remains still. (Much like my cousin Vinny after 15 martinis.) This behavior is called thanatosis. And while it won't get you out of paying the bar bill, it just might discourage predators that are too persnickety to eat dead stuff.

While female stick insects have learned to live without males, that doesn't mean they want to be stuck raising the kids. While some make a bit of effort to hide the eggs they lay, most just drop them randomly around on the forest floor and beat it, leaving the hatching youngsters to fend for themselves.

Fortunately, many walking stick eggs resemble seeds, so they're often ignored by most carnivorous creatures. Some eggs have a special fatty capsule on one end called a capitulum. Ants are attracted to it, and carry the eggs back to their nests. After eating the fatty capsule, they toss the still viable eggs onto their community garbage heap, where they can incubate safe and warm and away from predators. (And you thought ma didn't care.)

Fun Fact: Go big or go home. In 2008, a new species of stick insect discovered in Borneo broke the world record for the longest insect (which had previously been held by another stick insect). Dubbed the Chan's Megastick, it measures an astounding 22 inches with its legs extended, and has a body length of 14 inches.

CHAPTER 8
PRESIDENTIAL PARDON-ME

WORRIED ABOUT YOUR TABLE MANNERS? Hey, not everybody can be Emily Post. To put your mind at ease, check out these dinner disasters by people who probably should have known better.

While visiting San Antonio and The Alamo, President Gerald Ford was invited to eat the quintessential Mexican cuisine, tamales. While the press cameras rolled, he tried to take his first-ever bite of tamale—while it was still wrapped in the corn husk. Oops...

President George Bush (Sr.), and Mrs. Bush were once at a formal banquet in Japan. Surrounded by elite Japanese political and industrial dignitaries, suddenly Bush felt nauseated. Unable to squelch the urge, he turned to his left, where the prime minister of Japan sat, and hurled. (I bet the leader of the Empire of the Nascent Sun wished he hadn't sat next to the leader of the Empire of the Nauseous Son. No? How about, East meets Wet? Okay, I'll show myself out ...)

In 1979, President James "Jimmy" Carter also lost his lunch, but for another reason. As the guest of honor at an official luncheon hosted by Mexican President Jose Lopez Portillo, Carter tried to spark some life into the conversation. He jokingly told Portillo that he'd started jogging, having picked up the running habit during a prior visit to Mexico City, where he drank some water and had gotten a really bad case of "Montezuma's revenge." (A euphemism for diarrhea caused by drinking the water in Mexico, Mexicans can consider the phrase an offensive cultural slur.)

Fun Fact: As you might expect, White House meals often cater to each president's favorite foods. George Bush senior despised broccoli, and never served it. Harry Truman loved watermelon pickles, and even offered them to then Princess Elizabeth of England. Lyndon Johnson always served beef and steaks, whereas Dwight Eisenhower served turkey at nearly every state dinner. Besides two incidences in 2016 (a ham and a pork-belly canapé), pork has not been served. Ironic that "the other white meat" isn't popular in the White House, isn't it?

CHAPTER 9
A PRETTY HEADY TALENT

NOT MANY PEOPLE can claim as much fame as this lady who was born Hedwig Eva Maria Kiesler in Vienna in 1914. By the time she passed away in 2000, she'd proven her talents as both an inventor and a film star. Who was she? Read on and find out.

When she was 12, she won a beauty contest in Vienna. Fascinated by film and theater, she also loved long walks with her father, who spent the time with her in lengthy discussions about how technology worked.

Curious and eager, as a young teen she took acting classes. One day, she forged a note from her mother and went to Sascha-Film studio. There, she landed a job as a script girl. Not long afterward, she played an extra in *Money on the Street*, and was cast for a small speaking part in *Storm in a Water Glass*.

Have you guessed who it is yet? After honing her craft in a half-dozen other films, the ambitious young actress landed the role that would make her internationally famous. (But it would take another five years and a meeting with Louis B. Mayer before she changed her name to Hedy Lamarr.)

The movie that rocketed Lamarr to fame was the Gustav Machaty film *Ecstasy*. In it, she played the neglected wife of an older man. The film gained celebration and notoriety for showing Lamarr's face at the heights of sexual pleasure, as well as brief and close-up nude scenes. Lamarr, just 18 at the time, claimed she was duped by the director, but others contested her claims. The film caused quite a stir throughout Europe. American and Germany banned it.

Disillusioned with film, Lamarr retreated to Vienna and into the arms of Friedrich Mandl, a wealthy Austrian military arms merchant and munitions manufacturer. Extremely controlling, Mandl objected to her sexy scenes in *Ecstasy*, and forbade her from acting. Lamarr claimed he kept her a virtual prisoner in Schloss Schwarzenau, their castle home.

One bright note was that Lamarr was able to accompany Mandl to business meetings with scientists and technology experts. Here, she was first introduced to the field of applied science, rekindling her interest and latent talent for the field of science. The marriage, however, could not be resuscitated.

Years later, Lamarr would write in her autobiography, "I knew very soon that I could never be an actress while I was his wife. He was the absolute monarch of his marriage. I was like a doll. I was like a thing, some object of art which had to be guarded—and imprisoned—having no mind, no life of its own."

For a woman like Lamarr, that would never do. Four years after the nuptials, she split from Mandl. In her autobiography she writes that she disguised herself as her maid and fled to Paris. Others say she wore all her jewelry to a dinner party and disappeared afterward. Either way, their union was over.

Ironically, when Lamarr fled her castle, she ran right into a goldmine. In London, she met Louis B. Mayer, the head of MGM. He was in Europe scouting for new talent. Mayer offered Lamarr $125 a week. She turned him down, but booked herself on the same ship headed back to New York. On board, she managed to impress Mayer enough to secure a contract for $500 a week. He, in turn, convinced her to change her name to Hedy Lamarr, (partly to distance herself from the infamy of her role in *Ecstasy*).

Mayer brought Lamarr to Hollywood in 1938, promoting her as the "world's most beautiful woman." He hoped she would become another Greta Garbo or Marlene Dietrich. She did, and went on to make a myriad of films for MGM.

But Lamarr's off-screen life was quite different from her screen image. Often lonely and homesick, she shunned beaches and staring crowds. When asked for her autograph, Lamarr always wondered why anyone would want it.

When WWII broke out, she and composer George Antheil worked together to devise a radio guidance system for Allied torpedoes. The system used spread spectrum and frequency hopping technology to defeat the threat of jamming by Axis powers. (In 1997, both Lamarr and Antheil were jointly honored with the Electronic Frontier Foundation Pioneer Award.)

Lamarr also sought to join the National Inventors Council, but was told she could help the war effort more by using her celebrity status to sell war bonds.

Lamarr obliged, playing her role with a sailor named Eddie Rhodes. He would wait in the audience at every Lamarr appearance. She would call him up on stage, flirt with him, then ask the crowd if she should kiss him. After garnering a hearty "Yes" from the audience, she told them she would if enough people bought war bonds. After the bonds were purchased, she would kiss Rhodes, and the pair were off to the next war bond rally.

After leaving MGM, Lamarr formed a production company with Jack Chertok. Over the next 13 years, she would act in dozens of films for MGM and other studios. Her final film, *The Female Animal*, released in 1958.

Fun Facts: It's been said that Hedy Lamarr was so beautiful, people would gasp when they first saw her on screen. But she was way more than a pretty face. Here are some more interesting things about her:

- In 1953, Hedy Lamar became a naturalized citizen of the US at age 38.
- In 1960, she was honored with a star on the Hollywood Walk of Fame.
- In 2020, Austria put her image on a postage stamp.
- In 1997, Lamarr became the first woman to receive the Invention Convention's BULBIE Gnass Spirit of Achievement Award, known as the "Oscars of inventing."
- In 2014, she was posthumously inducted into the National Inventors Hall of Fame for frequency hopping spread spectrum technology.
- In 2019, an asteroid was named after her: 32730 Lamarr—not quite a star, but then again, Lamarr already was one herself.

CHAPTER 10
BE SURE & EAT BEFORE YOU GO-GO

GETTING INVITED to the White House for dinner seems like a treat not to be missed, right? But if you were invited by Franklin Delano Roosevelt, the food was far from delectable, even by Great Depression standards.

As the only American president elected to four terms, FDR played a deft hand of politics, but found daily chores a drudgery. When he won his first presidential election in 1932, he and his wife Eleanor struck a bargain. FDR would run the country, Eleanor would run the daily operations of the White House, and neither would try to horn in on each other's turf.

Unfortunately, as luck would have it, Eleanor turned out to be truly one of the worst cooks ever to occupy the White House. And oddly, for the First Lady, serving up bad food appeared to be a point of pride.

Why? Because the presidential couple had made a conscious decision to create budget-friendly meals during the economic woes that marked their terms in office. They saw it as a show of solidarity for all the citizens standing in bread lines and doing without during the Great Depression.

While the First Lady was an accomplished person in many ways, cooking definitely wasn't one of them. Perhaps it was because she didn't enjoy food as anything but a necessity. Her son James once said of his mother, "Victuals to her are something to inject into the body as fuel to keep it going, much as a motorist pours gasoline into an auto tank."

In hopes of making the White House a model of conscientious cooking during hard times, "First Housewife of the Nation" Eleanor Roosevelt declared, "I am doing away with all the kickshaws—no hothouse grapes—nothing out of season."

A few weeks after FDR's initial inauguration in 1933, the First Lady began instituting menus based on low-cost, but nutritious meals developed by the home-economics faculty at Cornell University.

One of Eleanor's first luncheons consisted of a main course of deviled eggs stuffed only with hard-boiled yolks mashed with vinegar and minced onion. The eggs were served hot, with a thin coating of tomato sauce. The sides? Mashed potatoes and whole-wheat bread. Dessert was a modest portion of prune pudding made from flour, water, and prunes.

For Eleanor, meals were planned almost as a necessary evil—a way to dispatch of two drudgeries (cooking and eating) as efficiently as possible. How else could one explain another of her standard menus; bean-and-tomato stew, fried liver with a slice of onion on top, and raw carrots marinated in diluted vinegar?

When Britain's King George VI dined at FDR's White House in 1939, he was served frozen cheese with watercress salad, followed by calf's head soup and terrapin (turtle) with cornbread. And they say British cuisine is bad ...

In all fairness, were she still alive, Eleanor Roosevelt would quite possibly have been an early advocate of today's "farm to table" movement. The only trouble was, she couldn't get folks to the table. Well, not *twice*, anyway.

When Ernest Hemingway came to dine in 1937, he declared the White House fare was the worst he'd ever eaten in his life. In a letter to his mother-in-law, Hemingway described the meal. "We had a rainwater soup followed by rubber squab, a nice wilted salad and a cake some admirer had sent in. An enthusiastic but unskilled admirer."

Journalist Martha Gellhorn (a friend of Eleanor's and later the wife of Hemingway) also attended the fateful fete he described above. Beforehand, while the couple waited at the Newark airport to catch their flight to D.C., Hemingway watched Gellhorn down three sandwiches. Gellhorn, who was a frequent dinner guest of the Roosevelts, told him that everybody in Washington knew the rule—when you're invited to the White House, eat before you go.

First prize? Dinner at the White House. Second prize? *Two* dinners at the White House...

Fun Fact: FDR didn't share Eleanor's austere palate. At mealtimes, he would often declare he was busy, and request a plate be sent to his room. (Makes me wonder if they had Uber Eats back then.)

CHAPTER 11
THE FASTEST WOMAN IN THE WORLD

LIKE PROVERBIAL "WALKING ENCYCLOPEDIAS," we all carry around a wealth of knowledge inside us—along with a history of our victories and defeats. That mix of knowledge and experience makes each of us pretty interesting characters, even if we don't show it on the outside.

Though you might've only recognized her as the little old lady in line with you at the grocery store, her life story was anything but trivial. Read on and see if you agree.

At the age of 82, Betty Skelton Erde still cruised around her retirement community in a blazing red Corvette. It went well with her ginger hair and her need for speed.

"An auto racing pioneer, Erde was once the fastest woman on Earth, setting female speed records at Daytona Beach and Utah's Bonneville salt flats," wrote journalist Tamara Lush in a 2008 article distributed by AP news.

Dozens of other records are attached to Erde's name. The auto industry's first female test driver (1954). The first woman to set a world land-speed record (144.78 mph at

Daytona Beach, 1956). The world land-speed record for women (315.72 mph at Bonneville in 1965).

Erde set those incredible records half a century ago. But when asked why she still drove a sports car, she nonchalantly replied, "I like fast cars."

But fast cars weren't Erde's first love. Planes were.

"To me, there's hardly any feeling in the world that can equal the feeling of an airplane when the wheels leave the ground," Erde said during her interview with Lush.

Born in 1926 in Pensacola, FL, Erde was smitten by the aviation bug as a young child, watching planes take off and land at a nearby Naval Air Station. She began taking lessons, and did her first solo flight at the age of 12.

"Unfortunately, it was kind of illegal, so I had to wait until I was 16 to tell anybody," she said with a laugh.

After high school, Erde worked a night job and rented planes by day. One day, a man organizing a local airshow invited her to perform. The only problem was, she didn't know any aerobatic maneuvers.

Undaunted, she learned to roll and loop a plane in two weeks. She soon mastered dozens of tricks. Her signature move was cutting a ribbon strung between two fishing poles with her propeller—while flying upside down 10 feet off the ground! By the 1950s, she was wowing audiences worldwide.

In 1953, Bill France, the man who started the NASCAR circuit, asked Erde to fly some auto racers from Pennsylvania to North Carolina. The next year, at France's invitation, Erde went to Daytona. There, she climbed into a Dodge sedan and, on the beach sand, set a stock-car record of 105.88 mph.

Erde had found her second love.

Fun Fact: In 2008, three years before she passed away,

Erde was inducted into the Motorsports Hall of Fame of America, alongside Michael Andretti and five other racing legends. She was also inducted into the National Aviation Hall of Fame in 2005. When asked to describe her life, Erde simply said, "It's been quite a ride."

CHAPTER 12
WIN ONE FOR THE GAFFER

WHO DOESN'T LOVE a good presidential gaffe? And nobody racked them up quite like jovial and charismatic President Ronald Reagan. Here are a few of his classics:

- While attending a reception in Brazil given by then President Figueredo, Reagan raised his glass and offered a toast, hailing "the people of Bolivia."
- Another time, when welcoming the Liberian leader Samuel K. Doe to the United States, he called him Chairman Moe.
- During another reception, Reagan greeted his Secretary of Housing and Urban Development with a hearty, "Hell, Mr. Mayor!"
- Believe it or not, Reagan's love letters to his beloved wife were addressed to, "Nancy Poo Pants," or "Mommie Poo Pants." (And they say romance is dead …)
- When he was running for governor of California in 1966, a reporter asked Reagan what kind of

governor he would be. The former movie actor is reported to have replied, "I don't know. I've never played a governor."

Even so, Reagan *had* played lots of roles. One of his most memorable was in the 1940 biographical film, *Knute Rockne, All American*. In it, Reagan played a star freshman football player named George Gipp. After leading the team to victory, his character is stricken with a fatal illness after the final game. On his death bed, Gipp tells teammate Rockne to encourage his team go out and "win one for the Gipper."

This phrase was later turned into a political slogan by Reagan. During the 1988 Republican National Convention, he told his vice president, George H. W. Bush, "George, go out there and win one for the Gipper."

Life indeed imitated art with that one. But art got the last laugh when the speech was parodied in the spoof film *Airplane!* (The film was released while Reagan was running for president in 1980.) In the movie, the main character named Rumack (played by Leslie Nielsen) tells a discouraged pilot to, "Win just one for the Zipper."

Arguably, Reagan's greatest gaffe of all was delivered in 1984, at the height of the Cold War. During this time, Reagan was known for his Saturday Radio messages to the nation. Once, while unaware the microphone was on, he jokingly said into it, "My fellow Americans, I'm pleased to tell you today that I've signed legislation that will outlaw Russia forever. We begin bombing in five minutes." Thankfully, the program was not yet airing and his gaffe was only heard by those in the immediate production area.

Fun Fact: The Gipper was not without his charms—wit being one of them. In March of 1981, Reagan was shot in the chest during an assassination attempt. Right afterward, Reagan joked to his wife, "Honey, I forgot to duck." While being wheeled into surgery, he told his doctors that he hoped they were all Republicans. If that isn't a star performance, what is?

CHAPTER 13
DEATH OF A SALESMAN (AS SEEN ON TV)

THE WORLD of late-night TV infomercials was rocked in 2021 by the death of trailblazer, Ron Popeil. As the founder of Ronco, throughout the 1960s, '70s, '80s and beyond, Popeil was both a pop-culture sensation and target of parody as he vied for our pocket money with his unique brand of gleeful, unabashed hucksterism.

If you've ever heard the iconic phrases, "Set it and forget it." "No muss, no fuss!" or "But wait, there's more!" you have Popeil to thank. And while the products he peddled on TV were certainly not necessities, charming Ron nevertheless convinced millions and millions of viewers they couldn't live without them.

Were you one of them? I certainly was. Ronco products often went viral before "going viral" was even a thing.

Popeil honed his salesmanship skills in his teens as a lowly street hawker, before landing a spot as a store demonstrator for Woolworth's. Every morning, he would buy 50 pounds of raw onions, cabbages and carrots, along with 100 pounds of potatoes. By the end of a typical 12-hour day, he'd sliced and diced his way through all of them—the whole while keeping up a charming patter with his enthralled audiences.

Popeil was only 16 when a Chicago newspaper called him "a silver-tongued orator." Before he turned 18, he was clearing as much as a grand a week demonstrating products at a Woolworth's store.

Mel Korey, who started Ronco with Popeil in 1964, told the New Yorker in 2000, "He was mesmerizing. There were secretaries who would take their lunch break at Woolworth's to watch him because he was so good-looking."

Popeil soon took his show on the road, traveling to state fairs around the country. In 1956 he made his first television commercial for the Chop-o-Matic. Coming in at 3.5 minutes, some say it was the first ever infomercial.

Both a salesman and inventor, Popeil got his ideas for products by refining items developed by his father and uncles, and by creating new ones on his own. The Chop-o-Matic (later renamed the Veg-o-Matic) was followed by such memorable gadgets as the Popeil Pocket Fisherman, the Smokeless Ashtray, the Buttoneer, the Record Vaccum, Mr. Microphone, the Cap Snaffler, the Electric Food Dehydrator, the Bedazzler, the Popeil's Pasta & Sausage Maker, Ronco Records, and my personal favorite, the Inside-the-Egg Scrambler. (I got one for Christmas one year.)

Knife sets were also a popular item on Ronco infomercials, including the Six Star Plus set. "You can slice a tomato so thin it only has one side!" Popeil would boast after using the knife to cut through blocks of wood and shoe leather. "Now how much would you pay?"

Perhaps Popeil's oddest invention was the GLH Formula Number 9 Hair System. Often referred to as hair in a can, it "hid" bald spots with a powder that, once applied, was then combed into the surrounding hair. Popeil himself gladly turned around to show his own bald spot and demonstrate how it worked. When interviewed by the *New Yorker*, he said, "People always ask me, 'Ron, where did you get that name GLH?' I made it up. Great-Looking Hair."

Undoubtedly, the most lucrative product on Ronco's shelf was the Showtime Rotisserie. Sales of the countertop oven totaled more than $1 billion. He told the *Boston Globe*, "My forte is mass marketing for big dollars. The product has to fill a need and the market has to be very big." He wasn't joking. When Ron Popeil passed away at the age of 86, he'd amassed a net worth of $200 million.

Popeil's commercials, with their over-the-top boasts, do-it-yourself hominess, and in-on-the-joke humor made him the perfect guest and foil for late-night programs such as SNL, David Letterman, and Conan O'Brien. Popeil was almost indisputably the inspiration for Dan Aykroyd's classic *Bass-o-Matic* sketch, in which Aykroyd pulverizes a fish to goop inside a blender.

Over the years, Popeil and his pitches were spoofed on such mainstream shows as *The X-Files*, *The Simpsons*, *King of the Hill*, and *Old School*. He was also frequently invited to guest on *The Tonight Show* and *Late Show with David Letterman*. In addition, Popeil's life has been chronicled on *A&E's Biography*, the History Channel, and *Lifestyles of the Rich and Famous*, to name a few.

Not bad for a teenage street hustler, right? Well played, Mr. Popeil. Well played.

Fun Fact: In 1974, Popeil's stepmother was convicted of hiring hit men to kill her estranged husband. She served 19 months in prison. Apparently unsuccessful in her criminal endeavor, the two later remarried.

CHAPTER 14
YOU'RE USELESS, I TELL YOU!

SIT BACK, relax, and reflect on what a genius you are. You might not have invented the microwave, or even the lowly lint roller. But then again, you didn't think up any of these stupefying inventions, either:

1. *Incognito Barefoot Shoes*. Do you love to feel the ground beneath your feet, but your demanding boss insists that you wear shoes to work? Incognito Barefoot Shoes are the answer! From above, they look like ordinary sneakers. But underneath their façade, like your mean boss himself, they've got no sole.

2. *The motorized ice-cream-cone rotator*. Do you consume such copious amounts of cones that your wrist can't handle the strain? Now you no longer need suffer. This invention twirls the cone so you don't have to.

3. *The walking sleeping bag*. Made of normal sleeping bag material, this nifty bag has vertical zippers on the bottom half that divide the bottom section into two independent parts, like a pair of pants. This leaves each leg free to do its own

thing in cozy, covered comfort. Now you can walk around without having to get out of the bag. You may never leave the house again!

4. *The DVD Rewinder*. Think about it. Am I missing something here? Be kind. Don't rewind.

5. *The Fish Walker*. This unusual contraption is basically a fish tank suspended over a rolling cart, making it more convenient than ever to take your pet goldfish out for a stroll. (Water and Goldie not included.)

6. *The Shoe Umbrella*. Sold in a convenient set of two for bipedal clientele, these miniature umbrellas fasten to the front of your shoes, freeing you to enjoy dry toes while you tiptoe through the tulips in the rain.

7. *The Butter Stick*. It's like an oversized Chapstick filled with butter. Fits snuggly in most pockets. Perfect for all those butter-related emergencies.

8. *Picnic Pants*. Imagine if maternity pants had a baby with 1980's rapper MC Hammer's funky trousers. Voila! Picnic Pants are born! Each fashionable pair comes with a stretchy web of fabric that extends from crotch to knee, sort of like the web between a duck's toes. When seated on the ground with legs crossed, the web stretches taught to create a surface perfect for holding snacks and stuff.

9. *Pet Butt Covers*. Embarrassed by your dog or cat's unsightly sphincter? Now you can cover it with a cute little flower sticker! The product description doesn't say whether they're reusable or not...

10. *Diet Water*. (Yes, it's an actual product.) Need I say more?

Fun Fact: On June 16, 1903, Andrew Jackson, Jr. (no, not *that* Andrew Jackson) received a patent for eyeglasses for chickens. Apparently tired of his chickens getting their eyes scratched or pecked, he developed special eyeglasses for them. They were made from two round pieces of glass fitted onto a front and back strap that held the glasses snuggly to the chicken's head. Perfect for any poultry Poindexter.

CHAPTER 15
WHAT DOES BLISS TASTE LIKE?

WOULD you like to overcome thirst, hunger, decay, and death? Sure you would! According to some yogis, all you need to do is learn *Kechari mudra*.

Say what? Kechari mudra is an advanced hatha yoga practice. It's undertaken with the goal of reaching inside your nasal cavity with the tip of your tongue—not through your lips, but from inside your throat.

Yes, you read that right. As you could imagine, for most people this requires more practice than getting into Carnegie Hall. Still, if you want to give it a try, here goes:

Okay, begin by rolling your tongue up and back and touch your upper palate. So far so good? Now, reach further back with your tongue until you can touch the soft palate. (This may take some practice.) Keep working at it, and you might eventually be able to touch the uvula at the back of your throat. Congrats! You're halfway there!

Now, unless you're Gene Simmons, it may take months or years of practice, but eventually, your tongue just might be able to extend beyond the uvula and enter the nasal cavity. If so, you're in the home stretch now! (Pun intended) Once there, the goal is to stimulate certain points in the naval cavity and taste the "nectar" which flows from the roof of the nasal cavity.

According to yogis, this nectar, or *Amrit*, energizes the body and helps one overcome thirst or the need for food. The taste of this "bliss nectar" is described only vaguely, as being sweet. That's interesting, as my bliss nectar usually tastes like a gin and tonic.

Fun Fact: Dedicated practitioners of Kechari mudra sometimes employ a "cheat" to make the tongue long enough. Besides months of daily tongue stretching, they also gradually sever the lingual frenulum (that little membrane thingie underneath your tongue) with a sharp implement. The goal of this long, tedious practice is to attain liberation in the body by sealing bindu energy inside the head, so it isn't lost. (I'll leave you to come up with your own pun here.)

Disclaimer: This story is for entertainment purposes only, and is not meant as a guide or instructions on how to seek your own bliss, either through your nasal passages or otherwise. You are a free-range human. Your bliss is up to you.

CHAPTER 16
THAT TIME THAT OLD LADY EXPLODED

IN 1951, two days before Independence Day, 67-year-old Mary Reeser unintentionally became the center of her own personal fireworks display.

Found by her landlord, Ms. Reeser had mysteriously ignited and had been reduced to a pile of ash. She'd left nothing of herself behind except for a bizarre assemblage of a few charred vertebrae, a chunk of shrunken skull, and a pristine left foot neatly burned off above the ankle, still sporting its silk slipper.

Until that fateful day, Mary Reeser had been a typical widow. She'd led an average pensioner's life, and lived in a very modest apartment in St. Petersburg, Florida. But her weird death would soon spark one of the oddest challenges the FBI has ever investigated—the case of the "Cinder Woman." It was so strange that even J. Edgar Hoover himself got involved.

During the initial search of Reeser's apartment, police discovered that the upholstered chair where Mary usually sat had been burned down to its springs. Mixed among the rubble, 170 pound Reeser had been reduced to less than ten pounds of charred remains—comprised mainly of her nearly unscathed left foot.

The level to which Reeser's bones had been reduced to ash was greater than is typically achieved by commercial cremation. Despite this, the police on the scene reported smelling no odor of burning flesh. Even odder, the rest of the room had been barely touched by the blaze. Oddly, a nearby clock had stopped at 4:20 a.m.

What the heck had happened to poor Mary?

Reports said that her body had been disintegrated by a blaze of "white-hot intensity." In addition, according to the coroner's report, the portion of the skull found had been reduced "to the size of a teacup."

Reeser's daughter-in-law offered the explanation that Mary had fallen asleep while smoking. "The cigarette dropped to her lap. Her fat was the fuel that kept her burning. The floor was cement, and the chair was by itself. There was nothing around her to burn."

All that may be well and good, but a simple cigarette igniting clothing couldn't achieve the 2500 degrees required to reduce Reeser to ash.

Police had their doubts as well. St. Petersburg Police Chief J.R. Reichert sent a box of evidence collected from the scene to FBI Director J. Edgar Hoover. Along with it, he sent a note that read, "We request any information or theories that could explain how a human body could be so destroyed and the fired confined to such a small area and so little damage done to the structure of the building and the furniture in the room not even scorched or damaged by smoke."

Despite the incredible length of his run-on sentence, Reichert eventually heard back from the FBI. Their pathologist reported there was no evidence of oxidizing chemicals or accelerants used. Instead, they declared that Reeser had been incinerated by the "wick effect."

The FBI hypothesized Mary had fallen unconscious while smoking and set fire to her nightclothes, which acted as a wick to keep the fire going. (Mary liked a nightcap and was known to take sleeping pills, but still, surely she would've woken up when she went up in flames?)

The FBI wrote in its report, "Once the body starts to burn there is enough fat and other inflammable substances to permit varying amounts of destruction to take place. Sometimes ... to a degree which results in almost complete combustion of the body."

The "wick effect" is a popular explanation, though no one has ever been able to reliably duplicate the results. And no explanation was ever offered as to why Mary's skull had shrunk. Interestingly, the FBI's official lab reports remain confidential to this day.

Many believe Mary was the victim of spontaneous human combustion. It's a theory that purports a person simply bursts into flames because of a chemical reaction within the body, with no external source of ignition apparent. Cases of alleged human combustion have been reported since as far back as 1663, and number over 400.

Back in 1745, a fellow named Paul Rolli was the first to suggest the possibility of internal combustion as the source of spontaneous human combustion. He noticed that victims didn't appear to have put up any sort of resistance. And often, portions of their limbs didn't burn—as if the main, internal source of ignition ran out of fuel before it could finish the job. Therefore, he theorized that the process must happen instantaneously within the torso.

Chief Cass Burgess, a detective on the Reeser case, told reporters, "This fire is a curious thing."

Yes. A curious thing, indeed.

The profile of the typical victim of spontaneous human combustion is plump, over 70, female, and prone to imbibe in alcohol, drugs, tobacco, or any combination thereof. But it can happen to anybody.

Anytime.

You're welcome.

Fun Fact: Back in 1966, Dr. John Irving Bentley was found incinerated to eight pounds of ash and rubble in his bathroom. There was nothing left of him but his charred walker and one lower leg, neatly burnt off at the shin. Oddly, Dr. Bentley's foot was also clad in a bedroom slipper, just like Mary Reeser's had been...

CHAPTER 17
BABY, OH BABY!

REMEMBER that old joke about the marathon runner named Willy Makit and his doubting wife, Betty Wont? Hmm. Maybe it's just me.

Anyway, if you're not happy with the name your parents gave you, take heart. Even if I'd been christened Mildred Picklepants, I wouldn't trade it for one of these. They're all actual names of real people. I swear!

- Toppie Smelly
- Chris P. Bacon
- Batman Bin Suparman
- Marijuana Pepsi Jackson
- Moe Lester
- Dickie Head
- Whet Faartz
- Sherlock Bones
- Kash Register
- Gay Neighbors
- Crystal Methven

- Lord Vol Demort
- Tokyo Sexwale
- Flavour Balls
- Tyrannosaurus Rex Mullens
- Paige Turner
- Hashtag Follow
- Tahra Dactyl
- Jurassic Park
- Phat Ho
- Holden Butts

Fun Fact: One of the earliest bipedal ancestors of man is named AL 288-1, (aka Lucy). A member of the species *Australopithecus afarensis*, in her heyday 3.2 million years ago, Lucy stood 3' 7", and weighed about 64 pounds. But how did she get her nickname?

The day she was discovered in Ethiopia in 1971, the anthropologists threw a party back at camp to celebrate. Someone with a tape recorder cranked up the 1967 Beatles' song, *Lucy in the Sky with Diamonds*. It played repeatedly, turning the unidentified pile of bones from AL 288-1 into Lucy. If they'd chosen another tune, she could've gone down in history as *Eleanor Rigby*.

CHAPTER 18
BROTHER, CAN YOU SPARE A BEER?

In 2022, Jimmy Carter turned 98, making him the nation's longest-lived president *as well as* the oldest currently living President of the United States. Even well into his late 90s, Carter still showed up to help build houses alongside other volunteers for Habitat for Humanity. If you ask me, this makes him a shoe-in for the most *humanitarian* president in living memory, too.

But while Carter devoted his life to public service, his brother Billy set his sights a little lower. On beer, to be precise. In fact, Billy's penchant for beer became legendary, as you're about to find out. (Actually, in some circumstances—such as a really bad blind date—beer could be considered a public service, couldn't it? Anyway, I'll leave that for you to decide.)

When Jimmy Carter left Plains, GA to take his oath of office in D.C., Billy took charge of the family peanut ware-house. His shenanigans quickly began to put dents in his brother's presidential reputation.

While Jimmy ran the country, Billy loved to hold court in front of his gas station, spouting such gems as, "Jimmy's still mad because I wouldn't take secretary of state. I want to be director of alcohol and firearms."

Billy was also quick to cash in on his brother's fame with paid appearances at prestigious public events, such as the world championship belly-flop competition. But his ultimate entrepreneurial gambit was the invention of Billy Beer.

First made for Billy by the Falls City Brewing Company in July 1977, each can was boldly emblazoned with his name in all caps—BILLY. The cans also carried Billy's personal words of endorsement:

Brewed expressly for and with the personal approval of one of AMERICA's all-time Great Beer Drinkers—Billy Carter. I had this beer brewed up just for me. I think it's the best I ever tasted. I think you'll like it too.

As a final flourish, the endorsement was followed by Billy's signature. During its production, Billy actively promoted the beer to the media and whoever else would listen, doling out such witticisms as:

"Paintings are like a beer, only beer tastes good and it's hard to stop drinking beer."

"Beer is not a good cocktail-party drink. Especially in a home where you don't know where the bathroom is."

"There is no such thing as a bad beer. It's that some taste better than others."

Unfathomably, in October of 1978, less than a year after production began, Falls City announced it was closing.

After production of Billy Beer ceased, advertisements quickly popped up in newspapers offering to sell Billy Beer cans for several hundred to several thousand dollars each, hoping to cash in on their perceived rarity. But since the actual *cans* had been produced in their millions, the real value was more like between fifty cents and a dollar.

At this point, one can't be faulted for thinking Billy Beer had been doomed to the dustpan of history. But no. It continues to live on in pop culture today. Check these out:

- In the 1970s and '80s, no fewer than ten songs were released about Billy Beer.
- On an episode of *The Simpsons* entitled, "The Otto Show," Homer pulls out his old concert-going jacket and finds a can of Billy Beer in it, forgotten from the last concert he attended as a much younger man. He pops the top and guzzles the beer.
- During the opening scene of *Daffy Duck's Quackbusters*, Daffy works as a DeLorean salesman. As a customer incentive, he offers a free gift-pack of ice-cold Billy Beer with every purchase.
- In an episode of *Married With Children* entitled, "Shoeway to Heaven," Al Bundy is dumbfounded when speaking to a reporter and asks, "Well, what happened in the seventies?" The reporter replies, "The Ford Pinto, *Diff'rent Strokes*, and Billy Beer."

Today, an unopened can of Billy Beer sells for around ten bucks on eBay. An unopened six-pack fetches up to $25.

Sadly, the colorful Billy Carter passed away in 1988 at the age of 51. His epitaph described William Alton Carter as an American farmer, businessman, brewer, and politician.

Some say that Billy's uncouth behavior was an unconscious form of sibling rivalry. (He certainly brought new meaning to the phrase, Carter's Little Pill.) But perhaps Billy was just trying to stay true to himself. As he once said, "I refused to conform to an image that a lot of people thought a president's brother should adopt."

That you did, Billy. That you did.

Fun Fact: Despite Billy's enthusiastic promotion of Billy Beer, in private he was known to have preferred Pabst. In a way, he even admitted this in one of his most famous quotes, "Yes, sir. I'm a real Southern boy. I got a red neck, white socks, and Blue Ribbon beer."

CHAPTER 19
DON'T HAVE A COW, SPACE MAN

LIKE THE POOR BOVINES THEMSELVES, it seems no matter where you go, you just can't avoid being sucked into the merchandising engine that now swirls around the theme of UFO cow abduction.

Everywhere you look, there it is: the iconic image of a UFO hovering above a field, a cow suspended in its glowing, conical tractor beam. (See book cover.) It can be found on T-Shirts, bumper stickers, TV shows, TikTok videos, Pinterest pages, you name it.

Do a quick Google search and you can find cow abduction lamps, earrings, an inflatable cow, and an inflatable UFO "fort" big enough for kids to play inside. There's even a magnetic maze game for children 6 and up called, *Invasion of the Cow Snatchers*. The manufacturer says it "builds logic and problem solving skills through fun game play." (Paranoia not included?)

Amazingly, you can even buy a UFO magnetic paperclip holder with clips shaped like cows. (I bought one.) Or you can purchase your own UFO cow abduction kit that lets you beam up a teeny-tiny bovine while spooky space music plays in the background. (Okay, I bought that, too.)

But how did all this cow-craziness get started?

Some say it dates back to an incident in Kansas in 1897. An article in the April 23rd edition of the local *Yates Center Farmer's Advocate* reported that on the evening of April 19, rancher Alexander Hamilton (no, not *that* Alexander Hamilton), along with his son and a hired hand witnessed a giant, cigar-shaped craft hovering above a corral near his house.

Hamilton claimed that in a carriage underneath the UFO were "six of the strangest beings I ever saw."

Suddenly, the men heard a calf bawling. They located it nearby, trapped in a fence. The rope around its neck was extending upward, as if being pulled toward the sky by some unseen force. They tried to free the calf, but were unable to.

"We tried to get it off but could not," Hamilton said, "so we cut the (fence) wire loose to see the ship, heifer and all, rise slowly, disappearing in the northwest."

The next morning, Hamilton searched for the calf and found out a neighbor had discovered its butchered remains in his field. According to Hamilton, his neighbor "was greatly mystified in not being able to find any tracks in the soft ground."

Hamilton's statement was substantiated by an affidavit signed by 12 prominent citizens. Each swore that "for truth and veracity we have never heard (Hamilton's) word questioned." Needless to say, Hamilton's story hit the press running. It was published in newspapers throughout the US and Europe.

Pretty convincing, eh? Now, fast-forward 79 years to 1976. That's the year an elderly Kansas woman came forward with a tale of her own. She said that a few days before the story was reported in the *Farmer's Advocate*, she had overheard Hamilton boasting to his wife that he'd made the story up.

It appears that Hamilton was a member of a "local liar's club" that delighted in concocting outrageous tales, the taller the better. According to the anonymous woman, "The club soon broke up after the 'airship and cow' story. I guess that one had topped them all."

Hmm… Beam me up, Scotty. There are no intelligent bovines here.

Fun Fact: One would think that a being intelligent enough to travel light years in space would have better things to do than pester cows, right? You'd hope they would be more interested in world leaders, or even the Kardashians. But one theory about why UFOs seem to be drawn to farms is intriguing: What better place could they find to test out their *tractor* beams?

CHAPTER 20
IT'S NEVER TOO LATE TO CHICKEN OUT

In 1890, in a four-room house outside rural Henryville, Indiana, a culinary legend was born. He'd just have to wait 50 years to figure it out.

When his father died when he was five, his mother had to work. She left him, barely beyond a toddler himself, to cook for his younger siblings. At age 12, he quit school and went to work on a farm, later saying that "algebra's what drove me off."

As a young man, he held a dizzying array of jobs, including streetcar conductor, army man, steam engine coal-stoker, lawyer, life-insurance salesman, ferry-boat entrepreneur, tire salesman, and Shell service station operator.

The last job stuck, and between pumping gas and changing oil, he started serving meals to customers, including steaks, country ham, and chicken dishes. Soon, however, he was involved in a shoot-out with local competitor, Matt Stew-ard, over the repainting of a sign directing traffic to his station. Stewart killed a Shell employee and was convicted of murder, thus eliminating his competition.

His reputation grew, and in 1939, food critic Duncan Hines (yes, *that* Duncan Hines) tried out his restaurant. Hines included a review in *Adventures in Good Eating*, his guide to restaurants around the U.S. The entry read:

A very good place to stop en route to Cumberland Falls and the Great Smokies. Continuous 24-hour service. Sizzling steaks, fried chicken, country ham, hot biscuits. L. 50¢ to $1; D., 60¢ to $1

Feeling he finally was on a roll, our determined restaura-teur acquired a motel in Asheville, NC. Four months later, it was destroyed in a fire. Undaunted, he rebuilt it. By July 1940, at the age of 50, he finally perfected the recipe that would seal his destiny. But alas, before that happened, WWII broke out. Gas became rationed and tourism dried up. He had to close his motel and take work as a cafeteria manager in Oak Ridge, TN.

At this point, most people probably would've given up on their dreams. But not our guy. In 1952, at the age of 62, he franchised his secret recipe to his friend Pete Harman, who used it to open the first official Kentucky Fried Chicken in South Salt Lake, Utah.

That's right. The man in this story is Harland Sanders—better known as Colonel Sanders. (Ten years later, his secret recipe, a blend of 11 herbs and spices, along with a unique method for frying chicken in a pressure cooker, would earn him a patent.)

How did he get the name Colonel? Back in the early 1950s, Lawrence Wetherby, governor of Kentucky, recommissioned Sanders as a Kentucky colonel. Sanders went with it, and began developing his iconic image. He grew a goatee and wore a black frock coat, which he later switched to a white suit. He also donned a string tie and began referring to himself as "Colonel." He never wore anything else in public for the last 20 years of his life.

While Sanders is credited with the secret chicken recipe, it was Don Anderson, a sign painter hired by the first franchisee, Pete Harman, who coined the name, Kentucky Fried Chicken. Harman himself came up with the phrase, "It's finger lickin' good." He also introduced the idea of the "bucket meal" in 1957.

While Harman's new franchise was doing well, all was *not* on the up-and-cluck with Sanders' own restaurant in North Corbin, KY. It began to fail after the newly opened Interstate 75 severely siphoned off customer traffic. Left to survive only on his savings and a $105 monthly Social Security check, the Colonel decided it was time to start franchising his chicken concept like a mad bantam rooster.

He scoured the US looking for suitable restaurants, often sleeping in the back of his car. He found several. And eventually, entrepreneurs began to seek him out, each agreeing to pay Sanders four cents per chicken sold. By 1964, there were over 600 locations.

However, the rapid expansion was overwhelming for Sanders. At the age of 73, he sold the Kentucky Fried Chicken Corporation for $2 million (the equivalent of about $20 million today). His contract included a lifetime salary, and the agreement that Sanders would be the company's quality controller—a job he took very seriously.

As a salaried brand ambassador, Sanders' influence over executives and franchisees was formidable. When he discovered a restaurant or company varying from what executives described as "the *Colonel's* chicken," they faced what *The New Yorker* described as "the force and variety of his swearing."

When the company changed the recipe for his gravy, Sanders spoke out publicly, telling the Louisville Courier-Journal,

"My God, that gravy is horrible. They buy tap water for 15 to 20 cents a thousand gallons and then they mix it with flour and starch and end up with pure wallpaper paste."

He went on to add,

"(The) crispy (fried chicken) recipe is nothing in the world but a damn fried dough ball stuck on some chicken."

A division of the company sued Sanders for libel over his remarks, but was unsuccessful. By the time of his death in 1980 at the age of 90, there were an estimated 6,000 KFC outlets in 48 countries around the world, generating annual sales worth $2 billion.

I guess you could say Colonel Sanders is the perfect example of that old adage, "If at first you don't succeed, fry, fry again."

Fun Fact: In a rather odd-duck move, in 2017, just in time for Mother's Day, KFC released a romance novella entitled, *Tender Wings of Desire*. Set in Victorian England, the cover featured a young, swoon-worthy Colonel. In the book, his love interest, the ravishing Lady Madeline Parker, "must choose between a life of order and a man of passion." The novella was made available as a free download on Amazon. (Even odder than that, several kids' bedtime stories about Kentucky Fried *Children* are available on YouTube, TikTok, and Facebook. I'm too afraid to check them out.)

CHAPTER 21
A VEGETATIVE STATE

DO YOU HAVE A GREEN THUMB? The folks below do, and theirs' might be as the Jolly Green Giant's. Why? Because they grew the biggest vegetables on the planet!

Love veggies or hate them, there's no denying these humongous vegetables are worthy of a prize—if not of a plate. Here are seven of the lucky winners:

1. *Cabbage*. The biggest head of cabbage rolled in at 138.25 pounds. It was presented at the 2012 Alaska State Fair by its proud grower, Scott A. Rob from Palmer, Alaska.

2. *Beetroot*. The heaviest beetroot was grown by the Fortey family in Cwmbran, (not a typo) Gwent, UK. Verified by Guinness World Records in 2019, it weighed in at 52 pounds, 14 ounces, "beet"ing the previous record held for 18 years.

3. *Zucchini*. If you've ever grown this in your summer garden, you might think you're a contender. But you'd have to beat Bradley Wursten of Holland first. He holds the world record at 206 pounds, roughly the weight of a dolphin.

4. *Carrot*. A dad from Minnesota named Chris Qualley

unearthed a fat, tangled mess of a carrot in his garden in 2017. Looking like an orange tornado, it weighed in at 22.4 pounds, shredding the previous record of 20 pounds set in 2014.

5. *Pumpkin*. In 2021, a man in Tuscany, Italy grew a truly monstrous one of these. According to Guinness World Records, Stefano Cutrupi earned the honor of heaviest pumpkin in the world with his record-smashing pumpkin. It weighed in at 2,702 pounds, 13.9 ounces.

6. *Potato*. Peter Glazebrook garnered world-wide attention at the UK's 2011 National Gardening Show. In a country chockablock with avid gardeners, he beat them all with a potato weighing in at 10 pounds, 14 ounces. That's more than a giant stack of 108 Mr. Potato Heads—complete with moustache!

7. *Rutabaga*. Scott Robb of Palmer, Alaska, took the prize for largest rutabaga during the state's annual fair in 2009. His rough-and-tumble root veggie was as large as a microwave and tipped the scales at 82.9 pounds!

Fun Fact: If you're ever in Boise, Idaho, you can spend the night inside a giant potato. The six-ton tuber isn't edible. It's the leftover spokes-potato of the Idaho Potato Commission's Big Idaho Potato Tour. The oversized spud sleeps two, and offers a chic, white interior. (Sour cream not included.)

CHAPTER 22
THE OTHER WHITE (OKAY, PINK) MEAT

READER ALERT: *In this article you'll find out everything you ever wanted to know about Spam, and perhaps a couple of things you wish you hadn't.*

In the 1990s, every second of every day, 3.8 cans of Spam were consumed in the US. That was a whopping 122 million cans annually!

Back then, people regularly and unashamedly chowed down on such delicacies as potted meat, Vienna sausages, liverwurst, and canned meats. Most were full of meat byproducts like lips, tongues, lungs, kidneys, livers, brains, spleens, blood, and … well, you get the idea. But you may be surprised to find out there are *no* meat byproducts in Spam.

In fact, this canned luncheon meat is made with only six ingredients: pork shoulder/ham, salt, water, modified potato starch as a binder, sugar, and sodium nitrate as a preservative. (Interestingly, that gelatinous stuff around the meat is formed while cooking the loaf in its tin on the production line.)

So, how did Spam come into being? It was first introduced

by Hormel in 1937 as a way to use pork shoulder, which nobody really wanted back then. (Oddly, nowadays it's considered a rather choice cut.)

Anyway, Spam got its big break during WWII, when it became a substitute for fresh meat for U.S. soldiers. The GIs joked about it, calling Spam, "Ham that didn't pass its physical." "SPecial Army Meat." And, "Meatloaf without basic training." But the last laugh was on them. Before the war's end, the military had purchased an astounding150 million pounds of the canned luncheon loaf.

War rationing and the Lend-Lease Act gave Hormel a chance to increase its production to the U.K., as well as to the Soviet Union as allied aid. British Prime Minister Margaret Thatcher later referred to Spam as a "wartime delicacy." In his memoirs, Nikita Khrushchev declared, "Without Spam we wouldn't have been able to feed our army."

During WWII and the occupations that followed, war-torn countries such as Guam, the Pacific Islands, and the Philippines also came to appreciate Spam. For the most part, people still do. In 1959, Hormel sold its billionth can of Spam. In 2012, it sold its eight billionth can. Today, the company offers 15 different varieties, from Classic to Jalapeño to Teriyaki. (In 2019, they added a Pumpkin Spice version. It was bound to happen.)

How did Spam get its name? That honor goes to Ken Daigneau, the brother of a company executive. He won a $100 prize in a competition to name the new product. What does Spam stand for? Hormel isn't saying. But they do admit the meaning of the name "is known only by a small circle of former Hormel Foods executives."

Hmm…

Moving on, where is Spam made? The Spam that's sold in

North America is produced in Dubuque, Iowa and Austin, Minnesota—also known as "Spam Town USA"—where you can visit the Spam museum, if you're so inclined.

Which state eats the most Spam? Hawaii, hands down. Residents of this island state consume seven million cans a year. Often referred to as "Hawaiian Steak," Spam is so popular there that both Burger King and McDonald's restaurants serve it on their menus. Spam masubi (sushi) is also a popular snack that can be found everywhere from grocery stores to gas stations. There's even an annual Spam-themed festival known as the "Waikiki Spam Jam."

Is Spam just an American thing? No way. Spam can be found in 41 countries on six continents and is served up in some pretty creative ways. For instance, in Puerto Rico, Spam is the main ingredient in a party staple called *Sandwich de Mezcla*, which is basically Spam, Velveeta, and pimiento spread served between two slices of bread.

In the Philippines, a former US colony, they use Spam in everything from fried rice to spaghetti. They even offer Spam gift sets during the holidays!

But perhaps the most interesting lovers of Spam are the once cannibalistic inhabitants of the Pacific Islands. They say Spam stands for Shaped Pork Approximating Man, and believe it tastes very much like long pig—a euphemism for human flesh.

As unappetizing as that may sound, there's no escaping Spam or its influence on our culture. It was mentioned in a song in *Monty Python and the Holy Grail*, thus leading to the musical film version of the production being named *Spamalot*. In addition, Weird Al Yankovic wrote the song *Spam* as a parody of the R.E.M. song, *Stand*.

Arguably the most memorable and lasting use of the word

appeared in the iconic 1970 Monty Python sketch entitled, *Spam*. It was set in a café that served mostly Spam dishes. Egg and Spam. Egg, bacon and Spam. Spam bacon. Spam egg Spam. (You get the picture.)

The word Spam was repeated so many times during the Monty Python skit that it led to the name being adopted to describe a growing new problem caused by the age of computers—namely, being inundated with unsolicited electronic email messages.

Today, we still call this junk mail spam. So it appears that, whether we like it or not, spam is here to stay.

Fun Fact: During WWII, Spam wasn't just for dinner. The G.I.s used the gelatinous fat in it to grease guns and equipment. The empty tins and lids made makeshift cutting blades, drinking cups, and containers. In fact, Spam paraphernalia became so prevalent among the troops that Uncle Sam was nicknamed "Uncle Spam," and the USO was jokingly said to be touring the "Spam Circuit."

CHAPTER 23
DON'T TOUCH ME—I'M NOT IN THE MOOG

THE SUBJECT of this article probably isn't what you imagined. Not unless you thought it was about the theremin, of course. If you're like me, you've probably never heard of the musical instrument. But have you ever heard one being played? I'd bet the answer to that is yes.

A bizarre and unlikely discovery, the theremin came out of a Soviet-sponsored research project into proximity sensors. "Sensing" its potential as a musical instrument, (See what I did there?) the theremin was invented in 1919 by Russian physicist Lev Sergeyevich Termen. (His name was later dumbed down to Leon Theremin for us Westerners.)

A strange instrument indeed, the theremin was one of the first attempts to use electronics to create music. About the size of a suitcase, the theremin creates an invisible electronic signal between two metal antennas mounted on its base.

Without getting too technical, players place their hands between the two antennae and move them deftly to "play" the invisible signal passing between the antennae. One hand is used to control the frequency (oscillation) and one to control volume (amplitude).

For onlookers, players look as if they're playing an invisible harp. The sounds created by the theremin are downright eerie—somewhat akin to a wailing violin. After fine-tuning the new-fangled instrument, Theremin himself took it on the road to show it off.

After touring Europe and performing to packed houses, Theremin decided to pack up and move to the US. He got a patent for his instrument in 1928, and with some of the best timing in history, he granted commercial production rights to RCA just months before the stock market crash of 1929. (Needless to say, the release of the RCA Thereminvox later that year was not a commercial success.)

In 1938, Theremin abruptly left the US. Many accounts claim he was taken from his apartment in New York City by NKVD agents (predecessors of the KGB) and taken back to the Soviet Union, where he was forced to work in a prison camp laboratory in Siberia. (So much for luck.)

Whether this account is true or not, Theremin disappeared off the map for about 30 years, eventually returning to the US in 1991.

What happened to the theremin in the meantime?

The instrument enjoyed a brief revival in popularity following WWII, but soon fell out of use by serious musicians because of the new, easier-to-play electronic instruments being introduced.

However, a niche group of electronic enthusiasts and kit-building hobbyists began experimenting with building their own versions of the theremin. One of the most notable of these was Robert Moog.

Moog began experimenting with theremins in the 1950s

while he was still in high school. He published a number of articles about building them, and sold kits that customers assembled themselves. Moog directly credits his interest in theremins for leading to his groundbreaking synthesizer, the Moog.

Today, though many theremin sounds can be closely duplicated by modern synthesizers, some musicians still prefer the original theremin for its novelty and unique expressiveness. So, have you ever heard one? You have if you've ever watched Bernard Herrmann's movie, *The Day the Earth Stood Still*, the Disney+ series, *Loki*, or ITV's drama, *Midsomer Murders*.

You've also heard a theremin in in action if you've listened to any of these songs:

* The Beach Boys used an Electro-Theramin invented by Paul Tanner for their 1966 hit single, *Good Vibrations*.

* Jimmy Page of Led Zeppelin used a variation of the theremin on *Whole Lotta Love* and *No Quarter*.

* Brian Jones of the Rolling Stones used a theremin on the group's 1967 albums, *Between the Buttons* and *Their Satanic Majesties Request*.

* Frank Zappa included one on his 1966 album *Freak Out!* and again in 1997 on *We're Only in It for the Money*.

Fun Fact: A person who plays a theremin is called a thereminist. The group Lothar and the Hand People were the first rock band known to perform live with a theremin in November of 1965. Lothar was the name they gave to their Moog theremin.

CHAPTER 24
THERE OUGHT TO BE A LAW

EVERY STATE HAS its quirky laws. My home state of Florida is definitely no exception. Along with the usual regulations to avoid general anarchy, we have some unusual ordinances that appear suspiciously specific. Here are a few of my favorites:

- In Florida it is illegal to fish while driving across a bridge.
- It is illegal to skateboard without a license.
- Women (but not men?) can be fined for falling asleep under a hair dryer, as can the salon owner.
- One is not allowed to break more than three dishes per day, or chip the edges of more than four cups and/or saucers.
- It's illegal to fart in public in Florida, but only after 6 p.m.
- It's against the law to sell your children in Florida. (Vacationers, wait until you get back home, please.)

- Even though it has a reputation as the party state, you can't toss dwarves in Florida either, not without getting busted, that is.
- Men can't wear strapless dresses in public.
- It's illegal for unmarried women to skydive with a parachute on Sundays.
- You can be drunk in public, and you can sing in public. But you can't be drunk and sing if you're wearing a bathing suit. (I mean, one has to draw the line *somewhere*, right?)

Fun Fact: The first law passed by the newly formed United States Congress after the ratification of the US Constitution was an act to regulate the time and manner of administering certain oaths. It was signed by President George Washington on June 1, 1789, and parts of it remain in effect to this day.

CHAPTER 25
PLAY THAT FUNKY MUSIC, WEIRD GUY

EVEN IF YOU'VE played in the Philharmonic Orchestra, I bet you haven't heard of these instruments. If you have, well, I bet you can't pronounce them.

1. *The Cross-Grainger Kangaroo-Pouch Tone-Tool.* Designed by a guy from Australia who apparently loves to hyphenate things, this instrument uses rolls of paper and a sequence of oscillators to produce sounds akin to a series of air-raid sirens going off.

2. *The Hornucopian Dronepipe.* (And you thought the first instrument had an awful name.) The collaborative brainchild of some folks at MONAD Studio, the Hornucopian Dronepipe was produced entirely on a 3D-printer. It's one of a set of farcical, post-apocalyptic instruments created for an art installation. Another one bears the even harder to pronounce label of One-String Piezelectric Monovioloncello.

3. *The Ocarina.* This wind instrument is a type of vessel flute, which means it's made of clay or ceramic. It's typically shaped something like an empanada or the head of a golf

club. Played by blowing air into it, the typical ocarina has four to twelve holes to produce varying notes. (You may recall, the ocarina was a favorite of French fartist Joseph Pujol, but that's another story ...)

4. *The Octobass*. The brainchild of genius and string-instrument aficionado Jean-Baptiste Vuillaume, the octobass is basically a monster-sized double bass fiddle. Standing a jaw-dropping 11.41 feet high, it is far too tall and wide to be played by hand. Instead, it operates via an elaborate system of foot pedals.

5. *The Hyperbass Flute*. Not to be outdone by the Octobass, this flute boasts over 49 feet of piping, making it the largest member of the flute family. The piping isn't in one straight line, however. It curves around like a gerbil Habitrail, allowing the flautist to reach its many tone holes. A relatively new member of the flute family, it produces "growly" tones, and is still being refined by its maker.

6. *The Pyrophone Organ*. Also called the fire organ and the explosion organ, as you might have guessed it's powered by combustion. In other words, in order to be played, part of the instrument needs to be on fire. Powered by gasoline and propane, the resulting explosions force air down the pipes for the waiting organist to use to make some fiery sweet jams, man.

7. *The Sharpsicord*. Invented by professional "sound sculptor" Henry Dagg, the Sharpsichord is a gigantic, pin-barrel harp. Reminiscent of the way an old Victrola worked, musical tones are achieved via 11 rotating cylinders, whose pins strike strings within the barrel.

Fun Fact: Next time you're at the orchestra, opera, or your kid's music recital, impress your friends with this tidbit of musical knowledge: The opening where a flautist blows air into the flute (commonly called the blow hole or mouth hole) also has a much fancier name—the *embouchure hole*.

CHAPTER 26
THE END OF THE WORLD, HOLLYWOOD STYLE

AH, 2022. It was the best of times, it was the *end* of times…at least as far as Hollywood movies were concerned.

In the past 50 years, Tinsel Town has produced at least seven worldwide disaster movies set in the year 2022. In these works of fiction, the fate of the Earth was in absolute peril. But in reality, it was the films themselves that were doomed. Almost all of them were complete catastrophes at the box office.

Here are the seven films, in chronological order:

1. *Soylent Green* (1973) By the year 2022, people are basically living in dystopian squalor, dependent on a company called Soylent for the bulk of their food supply. The food supplement wafers they produce bear the company's name, Soylent, and come in various colors. Shortly after the introduction of Soylent Green, the CEO of Soylent is murdered, prompting a detective named Frank Thorn (played by Charlton Heston) to investigate. Along the way, he discovers the source of Soylent Green. (Spoiler Alert: It's people.)

2. *The Dark Side of the Moon* (1990) A space crew on a

routine mission are out of luck when their own ship malfunctions, sending them drifting on an uncontrolled journey toward the side of the moon we never see from Earth. Along the way, they find a shuttlecraft that had been lost 30 years prior. The crew board the vessel, and are overtaken by an unexplainable, malevolent force. Is it the Devil himself? A beast from the Bermuda Triangle? It's never made clear. (That's why it's an *unexplainable force*. Get it?)

3. *Time Runner* (1993) Military Space Captain Michael Raynor (played by Mark Hamill) is duking it out with aliens during an invasion set in 2022. Just when he's about to bite the space dust, his escape pod gets sucked into a wormhole. He ends up back on Earth, but it's 1992. When he figures out what happened, he sets out to change history and avoid all this mess in the first place.

4. *Alien Intruder* (1993) Here we go again with the aliens. This time, the spaceship captain is played by Billy Dee Williams. Sent on a rescue mission with a bunch of ex-cons as his crew, they spend their time in computer-generated virtual-reality worlds, living large with their VR dream girls. A sensual alien invades both their fake VR worlds and their real world, pitting the men against each other like some Martian Lolita. Good times.

5. *Deathwave* (2009) Inspired by the real-life tsunami that demolished Taiwan in 2004, the setting of this film is 18 years later in—you guessed it—2022. Here, Thai scientists are working to design an alarm system to avoid another natural disaster. But faults in the program set off false alarms, causing the public to question its accuracy. Big mistake. (Don't go to that big festival by the beach, okay?)

6. *The Purge* (2013) The premise of this movie centered around a dystopian world where, once a year, all crime

(including murder) is made temporarily legal. Why? For the betterment of the economy and society, of course! One guy with a gigantic target on his back is James Sandin (played by Ethan Hawke). The patriarch of a filthy-rich family, in 2022 he has to stave off a blitzkrieg of homicidal purgers dead set on getting ahold of his lucky charms.

7. *Geostorm* (2017) Man has figured out how to control the weather with satellites. (What could possibly go wrong?) When a power-hungry politician tries to take over America by infecting the satellites with a virus, he sets off weather disasters around the world. The only people on the planet who can stop him are the satellite designer and Climate Space Station Commander Jake Lawson (played by Gerard Butler). I forecast disaster…

If all this has got you worried about the apocalypse, don't fret. We survived *1984* and *2012*. And seven is a lucky number, right?

Fun Fact: In 2015, a company named Soylent began offering vegan-based, liquid meal replacements, touting that "Soylent products turn a full meal into a one-step process with everything the body needs to thrive. Complete nutrition science-backed and sustainable." Today, Soylent drinks come in a variety of flavors and colors—one of which is green.

CHAPTER 27
DO-IT-YOURSELF MUSHROOM CLOUD

EVERY SINGLE MORNING, millions of people survive a self-made mushroom cloud. You could be one of them—if you flush the toilet without closing the lid.

You can't see it with your naked eye, but once you flush your toilet, a mushroom cloud of water droplets and fecal matter are released into the air.

Freed from their intended watery grave, these microscopic droplets rain down on every surface in your bathroom (and, depending on the velocity of your toilet, out into the hallway and adjacent rooms, as well).

The plume can last for hours. And one of the surfaces in immediate peril of contamination is your toothbrush.

I'll give you a minute to let that sink in.

If you've been leaving your toothbrush on the bathroom counter or stuck in an open-air holder, don't panic. Obviously, if you're reading this, it hasn't killed you yet. Your immune system is equipped to handle a crazy amount of germs. But if you're exposed to an E. coli cloud, bets are off. You could get sick.

What's an innocent, law-abiding flusher to do? Well, you can start by regularly cleaning your toilet and bathroom. And you can minimize the toilet plume's reach by closing the toilet lid before you flush.

But that won't stop every particle. Dentists recommend keeping your toothbrush at least six feet away from your toilet. But the best way to ensure fresh breath and poo-free teeth is to keep your toothbrush out of reach of the mushroom cloud in the first place. Put it in a bathroom drawer. Use a toothbrush cover. Or do what I do. When not in use, I keep my toothbrush in the freezer.

Fun Fact: Well before toilets were invented, ancient people frayed the ends of twigs to create "chew sticks" to remove food from their teeth. Later, toothbrushes were made from the stiff bristles of boars and other animals. The nylon-bristled kind we use today first went on sale in 1938, and was made with nylon yarn.

CHAPTER 28
THE BRITISH ARE COOKING! THE BRITISH ARE COOKING!

WHILE PAUL REVERE never actually uttered the phrase, "The British are coming!" during his historic midnight ride through the villages of Massachusetts on April 18, 1775, he might have done his fellow Americans a solid to warn them about the meals in store should Britain hold reign over the budding new colonies. Had we not prevailed, instead of burgers and fries, you might be sitting down to a meal of these British culinary delights:

1. *Mucky Dripping.* This is a type of gravy made from all the stuff left in the roasting pan after dinner.

2. *Toad in the Hole.* This dish is basically sausages cooked in Yorkshire pudding batter (similar to pancake batter). It got its name because the ends of the sausages sticking from the batter look like toads popping their heads out of holes. Pour the stuff in a pan. Bake it. Then cover with Mucky Dripping and dig in. Yum.

3. *Bubble and Squeak.* Traditionally served on Monday with leftover veggies from Sunday (as if Monday wasn't hard enough, right?). The instructions for this recipe are to basi-

cally dump whatever you've got lying around (potatoes, carrots, peas, cabbage) in a pan and fry it up. The name comes from the sounds cabbage makes as it sizzles on the stovetop. No word was mentioned about the sounds it makes after you eat it.

4. *Rumbledethumps*. A favorite of Rumpelstiltskin (I just made that up), this delightful side dish is made by baking cabbage, onion, and potato together in the oven after topping it with cheese. Bonus—you can used the leftovers to make Bubble and Squeak!

5. *Singing Hinnies*. Hailing from the northeast of England, these simple griddle cakes are made from flour, butter, currants (raisins) and sugar. The dough is rolled out, cut into circles, and fried. Similar to a scone, they got their name from the sounds the butter and lard make while they fry. And the hinnie part? That's how honey is pronounced in Northern England. (FYI, in Scotland, singing hinnes are called fatty cuties.)

6. *Scotch Eggs*. Despite the name, these treats hail from Yorkshire, not Scotland. Basically, they're boiled eggs wrapped in sausage, covered in breadcrumbs, and baked or fried. They were popularized by wealthy Victorians, who would take them on picnics and long journeys.

7. *Eton Mess*. This easy dessert is said to hail from Eton College, where the aristocracy of England attend senior school. To make it, simply fold sliced strawberries into meringue and whipped cream. (Don't drop it, or you'll have an *Un*-Eton Mess. Get it?)

8. *Welsh Rarebit*. It sounds fancy, doesn't it? It isn't. Just pour some melted cheese sauce on top of toasted bread, and you're done. It's like a sloppy joe version of a grilled cheese sandwich. Hailing from Wales, the name is a joke, dating back

to when the Welsh were so poor they couldn't afford meat (rabbit) so they ate cheese instead.

9. *Spotted Dick*. (Insert your own joke here.) This popular dessert is actually a sponge cake filled with dried fruits. Doesn't sound too bad, until you realize it's made with suet— the hard fat that collects around the kidneys of sheep and cows. So, what's up with that dodgy name? Well, lore has it that the "spotted" part is from the dark flecks made by the dried fruits. As for the second part? It's a short form of the Old English word for pudding ... puddick.

Fun Fact: When surveyed in 2022 about their eating habits, 83% of Brits chose fish and chips as their favorite meal. Given the offerings above, well, who could blame them?

CHAPTER 29
SO YOU WANT TO BE A PIRATE, EH MATEY?

ALL-RIGHTY THEN. The first order of business is to can it with the pirate talk, okay? No more "shiver me timbers," and certainly no "swab the decks, ye scurvy dog."

Why not? Because back in the Golden Age of Piracy (1650s to the 1730s) most pirates were rogue business owners, merchants and tradesmen—or they worked for a government. Besides, there was no time to learn pirate lingo. Once a person turned to this larcenous trade, they rarely lived another five years. Arrrrgh!

Still want to be a pirate? Maybe these facts will dissuade you:

Recall the clever banter and elegant swordfights in movies like *Pirates of the Caribbean* and *Treasure Island*? Fuggetaboutit! Most pirates weren't into small talk, and preferred sturdier blades like axes and hatchets, literally chopping each other to bits like firewood.

Walking the plank would've been the merciful way out of a dispute with a *real* pirate. More likely, the offender would've been keel-hauled. In other words, they'd have been tied with ropes, often weighted down at the legs, and dragged along the barnacle-incrusted bottom of the boat, which acted as a human cheese grater. Fun times.

Many pirates *did* wear eyepatches. But not for the reasons you might think. It wasn't to hide a missing eye, or to look cool. (Though, on Johnny Depp, it definitely *does*.) Pirates wore eyepatches to keep one eye adjusted to the dark. If you've ever had a flashlight shined in your face in the middle of the night, it's kind of hard to see where you're going afterward, right? Wearing an eye patch allowed pirates to leave the sunny deck of the ship and enter the dim belly below with one eye already adjusted to the dark.

Pirates didn't travel in luxury. A million times worse than the lowliest budget cruise line today, pirate ships offered no toilets, no air-conditioning, and no ice for your rum and tonic. Meat and vegetables spoiled quickly. Beans and flour got moldy. Fresh water developed algae scum. What was a hungry pirate to do? He turned to hardtack—a brick-hard, barely edible bread that usually came with a side of weevils. The only thing that didn't spoil aboard was alcohol, which they drank more in an attempt to stave off dehydration than to get drunk. Yo-ho-ho.

Pirate treasure was rarely gold, precious jewels, or booty calls. Living a day-to-day existence, most pirates set their sights on plundering for food, water, soap, candles, and a change of clean clothes. If they *did* get lucky and found some gold or silver coins, they typically set sail for popular pirate hangouts like Tortuga or Port Royal and blew it all on food, booze, and women. Setting aside a nest egg for later was a non-starter. As I mentioned earlier, pirates rarely had a "later."

Many pirates *did* have pets, however. And many of those were, indeed, parrots. Why parrots? Because they were practical. Sailing around waiting for something to loot could get mind-numbingly boring. Pets kept pirates company. But they needed animals that didn't eat a lot, so dogs were out of the question. Cats were okay, because they were small and could catch their own food (rodents) on board. Some pirates had monkeys, too. But parrots were preferred because they didn't eat a lot, the pirates could talk to them, and, in a pinch, they could sell the birds for good money on the black market.

Pirates didn't dress like swashbuckling dandies, with bandanas or big hats, and long jackets. A pirate crew was made up of all nationalities, so it's more likely they all wore sailor attire typical for the period.

Back then, being a pirate was a career, not just something to do until they died. It might not have been comfortable, but a typical pirate ship was well organized when it came to crew hierarchy. Captains were voted on, and each pirate had a specific job and was an equal partner in the ship's bounty. They could receive performance bonuses, and if injured on the job (and needed a peg leg) they would be taken care of financially.

Not all pirates were outlaws. Those who were good at their jobs were sometimes hired by legitimate and supposedly law-abiding governments. They'd set the pirates up to ransack other nations and attack enemy ships, basically turning these privateers into legal hitmen. Captain Henry Morgan was perhaps the most famous of these "legit" pirates.

Fun Fact: The number of pirates who growled "Arrgh!" is probably zero. So where did it come from? It's a Hollywood invention from a 1934 movie. Actor Robert Newton used it for inspiration when portraying Long John Silver in movies and on TV in the 1950s. Newton's English accent and exaggerated rolling of his R's became the pirate-speak we now think of in popular culture today.

CHAPTER 30
THE THIRTY-SIX MILLION DOLLAR MAN

FROM 1973 THROUGH 1978, the Six Million Dollar Man was *the* show everybody tuned in to watch on ABC network. Part science fiction, part action, the series featured USAF Colonel Steve Austin (played by Lee Majors).

Austin was an astronaut seriously injured in a NASA test flight. To drive home this point, in the opening sequence, a Northrop M2-F2 aircraft crashes. The accompanying sound track was created using sound effects from an actual crash that occurred at Edwards Air Force Base in California.

After the accident, Austin's severely damaged body is rebuilt with a bionic eye, arm, and both legs, bestowing him with superhuman vision, strength, and speed. Thus, our hero is born, along with the iconic phrase, "We can rebuild him; we have the technology."

After learning how to use his new body parts, Austin can leap 30 feet, and run upwards of 90 mph. His new eye has infrared vision and 20:1 zoom capability. His new arm has a built-in Geiger counter and the strength of a bulldozer.

Austin puts all these nifty gadgets to good use as a secret

agent working for a fictional government office called the Office of Scientific Intelligence (OSI). To alert TV viewers Austin is employing his bionic enhancements, scenes showing him performing superhuman tasks were presented in slow motion, accompanied by electronic sound effects.

In one episode, Austin is surprised to learn there's actually a *seven* million dollar man. Built as a fallback in case Austin bit the dust, the other guy, named Barney Miller, can't cope with the idea of being half robot. Unstable and going rogue, Austin convinces the OSI to "turn down" Miller's bionics to normal human levels, and they all live happily ever after.

One of the best-remembered episodes of the *Six Million Dollar Man* was "The Secret of Bigfoot." In this two-part episode, Austin encounters not only Bigfoot, but the alien visitors he protects. While pursuing the beast, Austin uncovers the disturbing fact that Bigfoot is a robot, and that California is about to be rocked by a major earthquake. I'll leave it to you to discover what happens next ...

Fun Facts: The premise of the series was based on the 1972 novel *Cyborg*, by Martin Caidin. Before the series aired on TV in 1974, three television pilot films were aired in 1973. The series spawned another popular show, the *Bionic Woman*. What she cost to create was never revealed. If someone wanted to rebuild Steve Austin today, it would cost them somewhere in the range of $36-50 million.

CHAPTER 31
WHO YOU CALLIN' BIRD-BRAIN, BUDDY?

FOR HUNDREDS OF YEARS, scientists believed that primates like chimps, orangutans, and gorillas took the silver medal after humans when it came to the intelligence Olympics. But new research suggests they may have to hand over their silver medal for a bronze once.

Who's the new usurper? Ravens! Research recently published in *Scientific Reports* states findings that ravens as young as four months old can perform as well on cognitive tests as full-grown gorillas and orangutans.

Who figured this out? A team from the Osnabrück Research Group for Comparative BioCognition. Led by Professor Simone Pika, the group hand-raised eight young ravens, then tested them using a version of the same cognition tests given to apes.

The test measured spatial awareness, ability to understand object permanence, communication skills, and learning ability. It was repeated on each bird at four-month intervals, from the age of four months to 16 months.

The results were astounding. At just four months of age,

fledgling ravens were already cognitively comparable to adult primates, especially when it came to problem solving. In addition, the juvenile ravens understood quantities, grasped causation, and demonstrated social learning equal to chimpanzees and other apes.

Ravens can even pre-plan for future tasks, a skill that requires the ability for abstract thought. Scientists used to think this ability was unique to humans and great apes. (Not even monkeys can do this.)

Pika, lead author of the *Scientific Reports* article, said, "We now have very strong evidence to say that, at least in the tasks we used, ravens are very similar to great apes."

But that isn't really news to many ancient cultures. The intelligence of ravens has been touted through Native American lore, Aesop's Fables, and even the Old Testament of the Bible. Here are some more mind-blowing things ravens can do:

- In the wild, ravens are known to use tools, and work in pairs.
- They can even hold grudges against other animals (including humans) who they think have wronged them.
- They'll also stop cooperating with fellow ravens if they see them cheating during group tasks.
- Ravens have been observed calling wolves to the carcasses of dead animals, so they can enjoy the scraps after the wolf does the hard part of "opening" the body.
- Ravens bury their extra food, and remember the locations of not only their caches, but their neighbors—so they can go back and steal from

them. They even make "fake" caches to fool other ravens.

Fun Fact: Ravens like to collect and hide shiny objects such as small pieces of metal, smooth pebbles, and even golf balls. No one is sure exactly why. If you'd like to see a clever raven in action, YouTube has quite a few fascinating ones well worth watching.

CHAPTER 32
AND YOU THOUGHT YOU HAD ISSUES

BEING AN AUTHOR, I found these facts about books and the people who write them to be truly fascinating. Being a reader, I thought you might, too:

Do you know which author *published the most books* ever? That honor goes to American fiction writer, L. Ron Hubbard. Between February 1934 and March 2006, this prolific sci-fi writer published 1,084 books.

William Shakespeare gets the honor of *selling the most books*. The author and playwright only wrote 42 works during his life (1564-1616). But through the ages, his books and plays have sold over four billion copies!

Who *published the most new novels in a single year*? That prize goes to Barbara Cartland. This bodice-ripper romance author holds the Guinness World Record—23 books in 12 months.

Who has had *the most books written about them*? Believe it or not, an astounding 15,000 books have been written about President Abraham Lincoln. The only other one with more tomes penned about his life is Jesus Christ.

Which book is the *number one seller of all time*? The *Holy Bible* gets credit for this one, with an estimated five billion copies sold. It's also the most read book in the world.

What is the *longest book ever written*? ONEPIECE. A diatribe commenting on the "commodification" of comic books. It weighs in at a whopping 21,450 pages. Its 31.5-inch long spine makes it the longest book both literarily *and* literally.

What's the *oldest book still in existence*? The answer to that is, *The Diamond Sutra*, a Buddhist religious text. Dating back to 868 AD, the book was unearthed in 1907 by Sir Aurel Stein, a Hungarian-born British archaeologist.

What's the *fastest-selling book* ever? That honor goes to the final volume of the Harry Potter series. The seventh book, *Harry Potter and the Deathly Hallows*, sold more than 11 million copies in the first 24 hours of its release on July 21, 2007.

Which is the *rarest book* in the world? That would be Leonardo da Vinci's personal notebook, *The Codex Leicester*, of which only one copy is known to exist.

Which country's citizens *read the most*? Surprise, it's India! They beat every other country on the map, logging in an average of 10 hours and 42 minutes a week of quality reading time.

Fun Fact: The *smallest book in the world* is entitled, *Teeny Ted from Turnip Town*. Published in 2007, it was produced in the Nano Imaging Laboratory at Simon Fraser University in Vancouver, BC. Certified by Guinness World Records, the book measures 0.07 mm by 0.10 mm. (The head of a pin is 2 mm across.) Produced in a limited edition of 100 copies, you need a scanning electron microscope to read it.

CHAPTER 33
NEVER FEEL LONELY AGAIN

IF YOU'RE like me and haven't had a date since the Obama administration, take heart in that fact that in reality, *no matter what*, you are never truly alone.

Why? Because every second of every day, you carry around as many foreign bacteria inside you as you do actual human tissue cells. That's right. According to the latest research, the average five-and-a-half foot, 155 pound person is comprised of 30 trillion human cells—and 39 trillion *bacteria*.

Sure, it sounds icky. But take heart. Until recently, a widely quoted 1972 study by microbiologist Thomas Luckey had lots of scientists postulating the ratio was more like *10* bacteria for every human cell. At least now we can breathe a little easier, knowing we comprise the majority of … well, *ourselves*.

Of course, bacteria numbers can vary person to person, and fluctuate significantly every time you take a poo. In fact, I encourage you to forevermore think of your daily constitution as "Doo-king it out at the Battle at the Bacteria Bowl."

(Yes, so now you're scarred for life like I am.) But hey, isn't it great to now know that something good can come from even the crappiest day?

Moving on …

In addition to trillions of bacteria, a majority of humans also play host to parasites. (And I don't mean our ex's.) It is estimated that 80% of us have some kind of intestinal parasite living it up inside our gastrointestinal tracts. They, in turn, have company, too, as they live alongside a whole host of other good and bad bacteria, and fungi. (See? You're a fun guy!)

How do parasites get inside us? With over 3,200 species roaming around in the water we drink, food we eat, and even the air we breathe, it's virtually impossible to avoid them. But the most common route of entry is what scientists call the "fecal-oral route." Yep. Feces from an infected person makes its way into the mouth of another person via contaminated hands, improperly prepared food, and unsafe drinking water.

Thankfully, most human-invading parasites are micro-scopic. But some are large enough to be seen with the naked eye. The most common four are round worms, pin worms, hook worms, and tape worms.

How can you tell if you're under attack by parasites? Symptoms include abdominal cramping, repeated diarrhea, indigestion, bloating, itchy butt hole (Especially at night. You don't want to know why.), multiple food allergies, unex-plained dizziness or weakness, and foul-smelling gas—to name a few.

On the bright side, next time you inadvertently release odiferous flatulence in public, you can blame it on someone else—your parasites

Fun Fact: Every night when you and go to bed, teensy-tiny Demodex mites come out from their hiding places at the base of your eyelashes and eyebrows. Virtually invisible, the usually harmless parasites have eight legs and semi-transparent bodies shaped kind of like a cigar. While you sleep, they throw a party on your face, supping up the oils and dead skin cells around your eyes. While they're at it, they also lay their eggs on you and, well, poop in your face. So see? You aren't nearly as alone as you thought!

CHAPTER 34
WHO CUT THE CHEESE?

LOVE the smell of soured gym socks in the morning? If so, you just might have the makings of a hard-core turophile. No, that's not someone who gets their jollies sniffing dirty feet. A turophile (pronounced TOOR-uh-file) is a cheese fancier—a connoisseur of cheese, if you will. And for some, the smellier the cheese is, the better.

Here are some of the world's most odiferous cheeses. They're "rank"ed in no particular order, because aroma, as they say, is in the nostrils of the beholder:

1. *Pont l'Eveque*. One of the oldest known types of cheese, this French delicacy dates back to the 13th century. Apparently, so does its smell. Don't put it in your fridge unless you want it to forever smell like dirty French laundry.

2. *Epoisses de Bourgogne*. A favorite of Napoleon Dynamite (I mean Bonaparte), Epoisses is so foul smelling it's been banned from public transport throughout France. Purported to have a sweet, salty flavor, it's made from raw cow's milk and its rind is washed with pomace brandy.

3. *Ami Du Chambertin*. Hailing from the Gevrey-Cham-

berin area of Burgundy, France, this cheese's aroma has been described as somewhere between "barnyard" and "putrid." If you can get past the odor, the flavor is supposed to be a sort of grassy butter and cream.

4. *Limburger*. Originating from the historical Duchy of Limburg, this cheese is mainly produced in Germany. The "fragrance" of this popular, stinky cheese is commonly compared to mushrooms, dirty feet, and ripe underarms. *Guten appetite!*

5. *Raclette*. Internet reviews for this cow's milk-based cheese from the Alps are infamous. Those daring enough to give it a try have left testimonials declaring it to stink of dirty feet and vomit.

6. *Pont l'Evêque*. That's quite the fancy moniker for a cheese purported to smell like mold, barnyards, and bacon. Some reports say it puts off such a stench that partakers leave it outside until they're ready to consume it.

7. *Stinking Bishop*. This aptly name cheese is made by Charles Martell & Son at their farm in Dymock, England. Made from the milk of the rare Gloucester cattle breed, it took first place in a contest to determine England's funkiest-smelling cheese. Judges described it as smelling like "a rugby club changing room." Interestingly, its name actually comes from the Stinking Bishop pears used to make the brandy the rinds are washed with. The cheese dates back to the time of the Cistercian monks. Hmm. Maybe that's why they lived alone?

8. *Vieux Lille*. This cheese is so vile smelling it's been nick-named "old stinker" by the region of northern France from which is hails. Not for the faint of heart, it's washed with a brine for three months until it becomes just the right level of "pungent."

9. *Camembert de Normandie*. Required by French law to be made only with unpasteurized milk, this unusual Camembert is fairly hard to come by. Loaded with chemicals like ammonia, sodium chloride, and succinic acid, it puts off quite a chemical-smelling bomb. Authentic Camembert has been described as smelling strongly of mushroom, with "hints of garlic, barnyard, and ripe laundry."

10. *Roquefort*. Banned in countries such as New Zealand and Australia, this is one of the most sought-after cheeses on the planet. Produced from raw sheep's milk and left to mature in caves around the tiny village of Roquefort in southern France, this cheese not only stinks—it can be deadly as well. Because the milk isn't pasteurized, consumers of the cheese run the risk of getting a listeria infection, which can cause miscarriages and death.

On that happy note, are you ready to become a turophile? You would be in good company if you were. Whole magazines and groups on social media are dedicated to the love of cheese. If so inclined, you can even apply to attend the Academy of Cheese and become a Certified Cheese Professional. To find it, just follow your nose.

Fun Fact: Why so smelly, Nelly? Cheeses develop their unique flavors with age. The problem is, without proper tending, they would just rot and mold instead of mellow. To avoid this, cheesemakers cover their newly-made cheeses in rinds, then periodically wash them with acidic agents like beer, brandy, wine, and even pear cider.

The goal is to inhibit bad bacteria while encouraging the growth of a friendly bacteria called *Brevibacterium linens*. (It's the same bacteria that makes your feet stink. Another mouth-watering gem.) Anyway, most of the smell and flavor created by these good bacteria remain in the rind—thank goodness!

CHAPTER 35
THIS BURGER TASTES UMAMI, BRO!

UNTIL RECENTLY, we humans lived with the concept that our taste buds detected only four distinct sensations: sweet, salty, sour, and bitter. However, Japanese chemist Kikunae Ikeda thought something was missing from the list, and set out to prove it.

He believed *dashi*, a broth made from seaweed and dried fish cakes, (yum) had an extra savory flavor that didn't fit into the other four taste categories. Through laborious lab work, he sought to isolate the molecules behind dashi's distinctive taste, postulating that there must be some kind of connection between the molecule's shape and the flavor perception it produced in human taste buds.

It took a while, but the Tokyo Imperial University professor found the culprit. It was the amino acid *glutamate*. It had been hiding in the seaweed all along.

Way back in 1909, Ikeda published a paper about his discovery, suggesting that the savory sensation triggered by glutamate should take its place as one of the basic tastes. He named it *umami*, a riff on the Japanese word for delicious.

But Ikeda's idea was slow to catch on in the scientific community. In fact, it wasn't until 1990 that umami finally got the recognition it deserved. At the International Symposium on Glutamate (I didn't make that up) umami was officially declared a distinct fifth taste.

In 2006, neuroscientists at the University of Miami isolated the taste-bud receptors for umami, further validating the existence of Ikeda's fifth taste.

It's too bad the intrepid scientist wasn't around to bask in the glory. Kikunae Ikeda passed away on May 3, 1936, at the age of 71. But next time you bite into something totally umami, you now know who to thank.

Fun Fact: Our sense of taste isn't entirely up to our tongues. Flavor is actually a combination of taste and smell. As we chew, we force air through our nasal passages where odors are detected by receptor proteins on hair-like cilia on the tips of sensory cells in our noses. (They can detect at least a trillion different scents!) These nifty receptors send neural messages to our brains, and, together with our taste buds, help us perceive flavors. If you've ever noticed that food seems bland when you have a cold, that's why.

CHAPTER 36
SOMETHING FISHY'S GOING ON

MOST AVID ANGLERS have some pretty tall tales to tell. But the real fish stories below have nothing to do with whoppers, or the one that got away. These are about what I call "Cracker Jack fish"—the ones that come with a surprise inside. And by "surprise," I mean some really, *really* weird stuff. Here are my top ten. (*Warning, a few are kind of gruesome.*)

1. In 1626, a fishmonger gutted a cod in Cambridge, England and tossed the entrails aside. A woman nearby noticed a piece of canvas protruding from them. Upon further investigation, she found a truly smelly manuscript wrapped in sailcloth. When shown to Dr. Samuel Ward of Sidney Sussex College, he identified the bundle as three devotional works by John Frith, an early Protestant martyr who'd been burned as a heretic in 1533. In a truly bizarre twist, Frith's works were finally published in 1627 under the tongue-in-cheek title of *Vox Piscis*, or *Voice of the Fish*.

2. An article in *Scientific America* circa 1847 relayed this weird catch of the day: "A catfish was purchased in the

Cincinnati market, lately, which, on being opened, was found to contain in its stomach, a silver thimble, a gold ring and a counterfeit dime, tied up in a rag."

3. Included in a 1951 *Ripley's Believe It or Not* column was the tale of an Arkansas catfish angler named James Price, who accidently dropped his dentures into Bull Shoals Lake. Price figured he'd never see his fake choppers again. But ten days later, he landed a 20-pound catfish that had swallowed one of his dental plates.

4 & 5. In April 2014, 64-year-old Norwegian fisherman Bjorn Frilund was reeling in a 13-pound cod when he noticed the fish's bulging gut. He cut into it and found two herrings and an adult toy inside. Now, you would think that such a bizarre find would be a one-off, right? Wrong. Richard Keslar of Shelbyville, Indiana was fishing on the Ohio River and landed a 20-pound blue catfish. Inside its protruding stomach he found a Nerf ball and a rather sizeable, well, you know what.

6. If you find those tales unsettling, an unlucky angler named Jerry Masterson was fishing off Tampa, Florida when he caught a stunning 80-pound Yellowfin Tuna. When he went to fillet it, he found the decomposing genitals of an adult male. Police were alerted, but the body parts have yet to be identified.

7. Yet another fish tale dating from 2014 entails the discovery of a different, slightly less gruesome body part. An angler fishing on Priest Lake in Idaho found a human finger in the belly of a trout he caught. He put the pinky finger on ice and called police. Detectives matched the fingerprint to Haans Galassi of Colbert, Washington. He'd lost it, along with three other fingers, when a speedboat tow-rope got

tangled around his hand while he was wakeboarding on the lake about eight miles from where the fish was landed.

8. Not long ago, a redfish was caught in Florida that was purported to have swallowed a snorkel. Amazingly, it had survived the ordeal. The mouthpiece had grown out of the fish's side and the skin had healed around it. The other end was sticking out of the unfortunate fish's mouth.

9. A 1992 edition of the *Reader's Digest* relayed the story of Ricky Shipman, who lost his wallet while swimming off a beach in North Carolina in 1972. Eleven years later, in 1983, Shipman was surprised by a local businessman named Gause, who owned a restaurant just across the state line in South Carolina. A friend of Gause's had caught a large Spanish mackerel near where Shipman had been swimming, and had found his driver's license inside, still protected by its laminate cover.

10. But perhaps the biggest fish tale ever told came from a pair of Polish fishermen. When they opened the belly of the monstrous, 12-foot, 410-pound catfish they caught in the Oder River, they found the remains of a dead Nazi inside. The fish's stomach contents included dozens of human bones and German WWII military artifacts, including an SS eagle insignia typically worn on the front of an SS dress hat. Biologists who examined the fish estimated its age to be between 90 and 110 years old. Further analysis of the bones and artifacts revealed they had indeed been ingested by the catfish during the 1940s.

Fun Fact: The biggest fish ever caught on a rod and reel was a 2,644-pound great white shark, according to the International Game Fish Association. The official IGFA-approved record is held by Alfred Dean. He caught the monster shark while angling in Ceduna, Australia back in April, 1959. Since great white sharks have become a protected species today, this record-breaking catch will likely stay unbeaten for years to come.

CHAPTER 37
I'M BACK, ALL THE WAY FROM BEDROCK!

EVERY KID LOVES DINOSAURS, right? Many of us got our initial introduction to the ancient animals by watching the Hanna-Barbara animated TV series, *The Flintstones*, while munching cereal in our PJs on Saturday mornings.

Most of the dinosaurs encountered by the series' main character, Fred Flintstone, during his construction job in the city of Bedrock were long-necked, barrel-bodied brontosauruses. (One appears as a crane in the opening sequence, while the closing credits depict Fred being served up a huge order of "bronto ribs" the size of his primitive car.)

But sometime during the 1970s, scientists decided the beloved brontosaurus was as fictional as Fred himself. Here's what happened:

The name *Brontosaurus excelsus* (thunder lizard) was first coined by a Yale paleontologist named Othniel Charles Marsh. After examining an enormous partial skeleton exhumed in Como Bluff, Wyoming, he described the new species in an 1879 paper entitled, *"Notice of New Jurassic*

Reptiles." In 1877, Marsh had also named *Apatosaurus ajax* (deceptive lizard) from a partial skeleton found in Jurassic rock in Colorado.

An illustration of the Brontosaurus skeleton was the first dinosaur "restoration" to be widely circulated, and helped the Brontosaurus quickly gain fame with the public. When museums started displaying Brontosaurus skeletons (the first ever in New York City in 1905) the dinosaur's popularity skyrocketed.

But in 1903, paleontologist Elmer Riggs determined that Marsh's two differently named skeletons actually belonged to the same genus. However, there were enough differences in the skeletons that they could be regarded as two different species of the same genus. Since genus Apatosaurus had been used first, it won out on the name game, and *Brontosaurus excelsus* became *Apatosauras excelsus*.

It took a while for museums to change their display cases, but by the 1970s, the Brontosaurus—the most famous dinosaur in the world—had been relegated to the dustbin of history. Or had it?

Researches in the UK and Portugal were working to update the family tree of diplodocid dinosaurs and sort out how many different *Dipodocus* and *Apatosaurus* species existed. After scoring 477 anatomical markers across 81 individual dinosaurs, they made an important discovery.

In 2015, in a paleontological comeback worthy of a *Jurassic Park* sequel, new analysis of the dinosaur skeletons suggested that the original thunder lizard was actually unique enough to warrant reclaiming its old name.

Yep. The *Brontosaurus* was back, baby!

Fun Fact: In *The Flintstones* series, Fred had a pet dinosaur named Dino, which acted much like a family dog. Dino was modeled after a prosauropod-like dinosaur called a Snorkasaurus. Though Dino debuted in the opening credits of the pilot episode, he wasn't mentioned by name until the first season's fourth episode, entitled, "No Help Wanted."

CHAPTER 38
THE TALE OF THE TAIL

FOR OVER HALF A BILLION YEARS, tails were the height of fashion for pretty much every fish, fowl, and furry critter that roamed the planet. Tails came in handy in lots of ways—from swimming to swatting pests to swinging through trees.

But then, around 25 million years ago, some of our primate ancestors suddenly lost their tails. What happened? Did they leave them in a cab? Lose them in a bar fight? Sell them to make a quick buck?

The tale of how we lost our tails is full of surprising twists. Let's start with Charles Darwin, since he was the one who suggested we used to have tails in the first place.

Back in the 1800s, Darwin was a renowned English biologist and naturalist, and is credited with the revolutionary idea that man evolved from apes. (Back in the day, this totally shocked his Victorian friends.) He came up with the idea while studying skeletons. He noticed that while both man and ape had no tale, they each had a tiny set of vertebrae that extend beyond the pelvic bone. Of this structure, called the coccyx, he wrote, "I cannot doubt that it is a rudimentary tail."

Since then, studies of fossils have shed some light onto the mystery of our missing tail. The oldest know primates date back 66 million years. They had full-fledged tails. Today, most primates and all monkeys still have them. But when apes appeared on the scene 20 million years ago, there wasn't a tail to be found in the bunch.

Scientists pondered this fact for decades. One of the first clues about what happened came in 1923. That was the year Russian geneticist Nadezhda Dobrovolskaya-Zavadskaya x-rayed some male mice before allowing them to breed with their fellow female lab mice. She noticed some had gained a mutation that caused their offspring to grow kinked or short-ened tails. Further experiments revealed the mutation had occurred on a gene labeled TBXT.

It would take nearly a hundred years and an Uber trip gone awry to figure out the rest of the story...

Fast forward to 2019. That's when New York University graduate student Bo Xia took a ride in an Uber and ended up injuring his coccyx. "It took me a year to recover," said Bo Xia, who was studying stem cell biology, "and that really stimulated me to think about the tailbone."

Curious to understand how apes and humans lost their tails, Xia studied how tails form in other animals. He learned that a set of master genes switch on in the early stages of an embryo's development. This orchestrates different parts of the spine to develop into distinctive parts, such as the neck and lumbar regions. At the far end of the embryo, a tail bud emerges. Inside this bud, a special chain of vertebrae, nerves, and muscles develop.

In all, more than 30 genes are involved in the development of tails in various species. Xia figured that our ancestors lost their tails due to a mutation in one or more of these genes. To begin his search, he compared the DNA of six species of tail-less apes to nine species of monkeys with tails.

Eventually, Xia discovered a mutation shared by apes and humans, but missing in monkeys. And he found it in the same gene identified earlier by the Russian geneticist. It was gene TBXT. But the mutation he discovered had never been observed before. It involved 300 "letters" in the middle of the TBXT gene. The mutated version was virtually identical in apes and humans.

Xia took his findings to his supervisors to see what they thought of the discovery. One of them, Itai Yanai, said, "I nearly fell off my chair, because it is just a stunning result."

Good thing he didn't. Yanai might have injured his coccyx.

Fun Fact: Before you were born, you used to have a tail. During the early stages of embryonic growth, humans have tails—including vertebrae! But after about eight weeks, they disappear during a process called apoptosis. (It's a type of pre-programmed cell death.) What remains is three or four vertebrae that form the coccyx, also known as the tailbone. Fewer than 40 cases of humans being born with a true tail have been reported in literature.

CHAPTER 39
FEELING CRABBY?

IF you ever had a pet hermit crab, the thing you probably remember most about it was the smell it emitted postmortem. (Or maybe that's just me.) Ahh, sweet memories. Well, maybe not *that* sweet...

Anyway, did you know that hermit crabs aren't the lonely, antisocial little guys their name suggests? Quite the opposite. Hermit crabs are pretty outgoing, and like to hang out in a crowd—typically in groups of a hundred or more.

Interestingly, hermit crabs are more like lobsters than crabs. While the front of their bodies are covered in a hard exoskeleton like normal crabs, their lobster-like tail isn't. To cover their soft, vulnerable rear-ends, they have to scrounge around for a discarded mollusk shell to tuck it into.

In all, there are around 11,000 different kinds of hermit crabs. They belong to the Pajuroidea superfamily, which sounds kind of posh, considering they have to bum their living quarters from dead snails. Hermit crabs can be found in shallow waters around the globe. Most live in saltwater. But a few are semi-terrestrial, living part-time on land.

The hermit crabs most commonly found in pet stores are Purple Pincers (*Coenobita clypeatus*). One of the hardiest of the hermit species, they originate from the Caribbean, where they spend most of their time climbing trees, drinking rum, and burrowing under tree roots. (Okay, I made up the rum part.)

Hermit crabs communicate by emitting soft, high-pitch chirps similar to a frog. Often they chirp when startled, or to sort out territorial disputes with other hermit crabs.

Hermit crabs grow, but the shells they've stuck their butts in don't. What's a crab to do when it's grown too big for its britches? Well, the little creatures have worked out an amazingly intelligent and orderly system. They line up and shell swap.

When a group of hermit crabs come across an empty shell, they form an orderly line for their crack at trying it on. The line is based on size, with the biggest crab getting the first shot. If his derriere doesn't fit in the shell, it's passed down to the next biggest crab, and so on down the line until, like Cinderella, the shell finds its perfect mate.

- Interestingly, if a hermit crab can't find a big enough shell, it can shrink its body to fit. (If only I could do this with my favorite jeans.)
- Hermit crabs hold tight to their shells by pressing their abdomens and fourth and fifth pairs of legs against the shell's inner wall by contracting its longitudinal muscles.
- A healthy hermit crab smells like maple syrup.
- A crab that smells a bit like eggs could be getting ready to molt.

Besides having to deal with outgrowing their homes,

hermit crabs also have to molt their skins to grow. When a hermit crab gets too big for its exoskeleton (hard outer skin) it has to shed it and develop a new one. To do this, the crab kind of turns into the *Incredible Hulk*, building up water pressure inside its body until the force splits open its exoskeleton.

After molting, a hermit crab's new exoskeleton takes about a week to harden. Meanwhile, the vulnerable crab holes up somewhere to hide out and munch on its shed exoskeleton, possibly to reabsorb important minerals to strengthen their new one. You can tell a crab is freshly molted if it has a clean, bluish color. Once grown, a hermit crab generally molts once a year.

Hermit crabs come in a range of sizes, from a fraction of an inch to nearly the size of a coconut. They all come equipped with a pair of eyes on stalks, and have acute vision.

Nocturnal scavengers, the crabs employ a short, feathery pair of antennae for smelling and tasting. And when it comes to chowing down, they're not picky. Voracious omnivores, they'll eat just about anything their little pincers can get ahold of, live or dead.

Fun Fact: In the wild, the life of a hermit crab is usually pretty brief. (Perhaps from all those crowd parties and eating dead stuff.) But in captivity, hermit crabs can live up to 40 years. Captive hermit crabs have been known to enjoy fiddling around with children's building blocks, exploring dollhouses, and even taking a turn at obstacle courses created for them.

CHAPTER 40
AND YOU THINK YOUR JOB SUCKS

COMPARED to folks in earlier times, we lead the cushiest lives ever. Especially when it comes to the work we do to eke out a living. Even having to clean public toilets would be a walk in the park compared to the tasks you'll find in this dirty dozen collection of the worst jobs in history. (FYI, don't read this while you're eating, okay?)

1. *Groom of the Stool*. Back in the times when kings were considered chosen by divine right and on the level of gods, it was thought they were too heavenly to wipe their own bottoms. That's where the Groom of the Stool comes in. Job duties included fetching the king's toilet chair, wiping his derriere, and collecting his stool for examination in order to monitor his health. And, should the glorious occasion arise that the king became constipated, the Groom of the Stool was there to administer his enema.

2. *Medieval Barber*. Back then, a barber didn't just cut hair. He also had to perform amputations, pull teeth, give enemas, perform primitive surgeries, and administer blood-

letting. Did I mention he had to do it all without anesthesia? Fun times.

3. *Vomit collector.* During Roman times, the elite would hold feasts called bacchanal. There they would eat, drink, and be merry until they could eat, drink and be merry no more. To keep the feast going, they would purge themselves, either into receptacles or on the floor. Then the handy dandy Vomit Collector would spring into action. After all, the party must go on …

4. *Gong Farmer.* Doesn't sound too bad, until you find out what they're "harvesting." Gong Farmers spent their nights fishing through cesspits and privies with nets and sieved ladles, cleaning out the waste left by their human customers. Not only did the job pose lethal dangers from gases and germs. The whole process left them so smelly Gong Farmers were often restricted as to where they could live.

5. *Leech Collector.* In the Middle Ages, blood-letting methods were often prescribed as cures for a multitude of medical ailments. One way to let blood was by applying leeches to the skin. These, of course, had to be gathered from ponds and bogs. The blood-sucking creatures were too hard to spot and trap with nets, so Leech Collectors used their own bodies as bait. They would enter the water bare legged and wade around until the leeches attached to them. After they'd "collected" a batch, they would then pull them off and sell them to local doctors, barber-surgeons, and other so-called "medical professionals."

6. *Rat Catcher.* The industrial boom of the 1800s had people flocking to cities for jobs. But humans weren't the only ones looking to cash in on the bonanza. Rats followed them, and found an easy life among the burgeoning piles of waste and garbage. Whenever the rodents got to be too many to

handle, the Rat Catcher came to the rescue. Problem was, rats were hard to catch. So the Rat Catcher rubbed oils like thyme and aniseed into his hands and clothing to attract them. Once within reach, he'd grab them with his bare hands.

7. *Fuller*. Back in the Middle Ages, people wore a lot of wool. The problem was, cloth made from raw wool is coarse, wide-meshed, and frays easily. To solve these problems, the sheep grease needed to be removed from the fabric. Unfortunately for the Fuller, this meant soaking the wool in a tub of stale urine, and stomping around on it for hours on end. Not only that, a Fuller often had to collect the urine required for his task from private households and public toilets.

8. *Executioner/Cleaner*. Executions, torture, and public whippings were popular in medieval times, giving the person who held this job plenty of job security. But not only did this fellow have to dispatch his victims—he also had to carry them away and clean up everything afterward.

9. *Plague Worker*. Like a scene out of a *Monty Python* movie, this poor fellow had to go around with a cart collecting the dead to be thrown into burial pits. Whether or not he walked around shouting, "Bring out your dead!" is perhaps a fact lost to history.

10. *Bone Grubber*. In Victorian cities, scavenging was an important part of the economy. The Bone Gruber would go around scavenging smelly bones from butchers, fly-infested garbage piles, and blood-soaked stockyards. They would sell the bones to dealers, who resold them to businesses that used them to make such cringe-worthy items as toothbrush handles and children's teething rings. What couldn't be sold was boiled down to be used in making soap, or ground into fertilizer.

11. *Violin String Maker*. That doesn't sound so bad, right?

But prior to the 17th century, the process was quite disgusting. In order to make violin strings thick enough to play lower notes, the preferred method required twisting strands of sheep innards together. String Makers had to be meticulous when butchering the sheep so as not to rupture the lower intestines or stomach. Then they had to soak the guts in wood ash, dry them, and twist them into strings.

12. *Tanner*. Perhaps the most repulsive job of the lot, a Victorian-era Tanner was charged with preserving hides from cattle, pigs, and other animals for use in making manufactured goods. The process involved soaking the hides in lime pits to soften the tissues and hide hair. Then the hair and fat had to be scraped off by hand. The "cleaned" hide was then immersed in a vat of water and dog poop (no, I didn't make that up) to further cleanse and soften it. The job was ongoing, and so was the fetidness of the fermenting vats and pits used in the process. (And you thought the stench from someone reheating their fish dinner in the microwave was bad.)

Fun Fact: Another job that's gone out of fashion is the Cup Bearer. It used to be an important position in royal courts, as it was the person who served the reigning monarch their drinks. A king had to have complete trust in their Cup Bearer, so it was quite an influential position in court politics. The only drawback was, the Cup Bearer was responsible for making sure the drinks he served weren't poisoned. Often, that required tasting any suspicious beverages himself.

CHAPTER 41
ALIEN APPLE INVASION ALERT

REMEMBER how killer bees and murder hornets were going to take over the world? It appears all that buzz was a tad exaggerated. But there *is* one alien invader that's leaving a slow, silent, and potentially deadly trail across the planet—including southern parts of the US.

The culprit? A freshwater mollusk known as the apple snail. Native to South America, the snail got its name from the shape of its shell and its size. Adults can grow to be as big as a mature apple!

In 1980, apple snails were introduced to Taiwan as a potential food source. However, the snails quickly got out of hand, eating everything they could slime their way onto, including the country's valued rice crops. Before long, they were popping up in China, Cambodia, Thailand, and Japan.

Since then, several species of these crafty snails have made their way into other parts of Asia, Europe, Central America, and North America. They're now considered a major pest of rice crops in Spain, Southeast Asia, the Philippines, and Central America, where they gobble up young, seedling rice.

But that isn't all that's on the menu for these voracious snails. They aren't picky eaters above or under the water. Apple snails consume huge amounts of subaquatic vegetation, destroying habitat for fish and other aquatic animals. They also consume the eggs of frogs and other amphibians. (Told you they weren't picky.)

If that weren't bad enough, Apple snails reproduce faster than memes on the internet! The telltale sign they've made it to your neighborhood are their neon-pink egg masses. They lay them on plant stalks like cattails and pickerel weed that protrude from fresh-water ponds and lakes.

The apple snail currently plaguing the Gulf Coast of the US is the *Pomacea maculata*. It showed up in Louisiana more than a decade ago in freshwater bayous, swamps, ponds and lakes. In 2018, the state's crawfish and rice farmers began reporting the snails in their agricultural ponds. California and Texas have also felt the effects of this pest's slimy invasion.

So, how can the apple snail be thwarted? The answer is, drill, baby, drill! Not for oil, but for seed beds. Say what?

Drill-seeding is the practice of planting rice kernels in seed beds drilled into dry earth. This foils the apple snails' plans, as they need moisture to survive. Around five weeks after planting, the rice fields are permanently flooded. The practice appears to have mitigated the snails' impact on Texas rice, and is working in Louisiana as well.

But apple snails are still posing a dire problem for Louisiana's crawfish farmers. The creatures are attracted to the bait used in crawfish traps, both filling the traps and blocking entry into them for the intended catch. At some farms, so many apple snails are trapped that they have problems finding places to dispose of them!

You might be thinking, hey! I've got an idea. Why don't we eat them, like escargot? Well, sure. But doing so is like playing Russian roulette with your gut.

Apple snails are *indeed* edible, but only when properly cleaned (including removing all of their intestinal material) and then thoroughly cooked. Raw or underdone snails carry rat lungworm (*Angiostrongylus cantonensis*)—a parasite that can cause potentially fatal eosinophilic meningitis.

How about snail caviar? Nope. Those hot-pink eggs they lay contain a neurotoxin called PcPV2. It can be lethal to small animals like mice, and can cause skin and eye irritation in humans.

Fun Fact: If you happen to spot a bright-pink clutch of apple snail eggs, don't touch them. Find a stick or something and knock them into the water. Ironically, like the cackling green witch in *The Wizard of Oz*, water is deadly to the snails' unhatched eggs.

CHAPTER 42
WHO KNEW WE WERE SO RICH?

Ah, there's nothing more valuable than spending time with the family, right? But we wouldn't have any relatives in the first place if our fathers didn't have a set of "family jewels."

Slang for the distinctly male part of the human anatomy, the term was first coined in the Victorian era as a euphemism for a man's ability to procreate. Today, the phrase is more popular than ever. And it's been used to name some rather surprising things besides, well, you know what.

Here's a quick look at some of the most notable uses of the term "family jewels" in print, film, music, and pop culture:

- A set of reports detailing illegal, inappropriate, and otherwise "sensitive" activities conducted by the US Central Intelligence Agency (CIA). (Yes, they were actually entitled, *Family Jewels.*)
- A 1965 film starring Jerry Lewis.
- The name of a 1990s rock band, as well as the album they released.
- A 2003 album by Foghat. (Family Joules.)

- An album released in 2010 by Marina and the Diamonds.
- A two-disc compilation DVD by rock band AC/DC, featuring music videos and live clips shot between 1975-1991.
- An American reality TV series featuring Gene Simmons, bassist and vocalist for the rock band Kiss.

Fun Fact: The show, *Gene Simmons Family Jewels*, premiered in 2006 and ran for seven seasons. (In its second season, it was the highest rated show on the A&E network, being topped only by *Dog the Bounty Hunter*.)

The show starred Gene Simmons, his wife Shannon Tweed, and their two children, Nick and Sophie. Simmons described the show as being "Very much like *The Osbournes*. But I believe that people will see us on television and see how I run things and the rules I make, and they'll think, 'Put that guy in charge!'"

CHAPTER 43
DOGGONE LOYAL PETS

IN A PERFECT WORLD, we all have that certain someone we can count on to be there for us no matter what. For some, it's a human. For others, it's a pet. Dogs are frequently touted as being the most loyal of companions. But can other animals bond with humans and show devotion, too?

The answer is yes. And you may find the animals capable of it quite surprising! Take a look at these atypical, but true-at-heart pets:

1. *Rabbits*. Soft, cuddly and surprisingly clean, bunnies are quite adaptable to humans and their lifestyles. One tale of loyalty is the account of a rescued cottontail rabbit. When released back into the wild, it returned almost daily to spend time with the woman who had shared her home and cared for it for over a year. After being freed, the rabbit actually sought out her companionship for months, even though it had made friends with at least three other wild cottontails.

2. *Goats*. Research has discovered evidence that goats are as clever as dogs, and just as capable of building emotional relationships. And, like dogs, one way they display that

loyalty by standing by their owners and staring intensely as their human struggles to complete some tasks at hand. Whether goats find it interesting or are trying to lend emotional support, it's not certain. But either way, it's a companionable trait once thought to be performed only by domesticated dogs.

3. *Guinea Pigs*. These small, good-natured vegetarians are quite content with a nice meal and a long nap. Easy to keep, they are happy to see you. (Some even emit a squeak of delight when you enter the room.) They like to cuddle. And some will even actively engage in a game of "who gets the short end of the straw," as you both nibble away at opposite ends of a carrot or leafy green, just like the spaghetti scene from the animated Disney movie, *Lady and the Tramp*.

4. *Ducks*. They may not the first animal that springs to mind when you think of a loyal companion, right? But thanks to the phenomenon of imprinting, ducklings can form incredibly deep bonds with the humans who raise them. Imprinted ducks will spend the rest of their lives seeking the love and attention of their surrogate mothers. Playful and energetic, duck owners describe them as being somewhere between puppies and children. This sounds pretty apropos, considering bonded ducks will forever view you as their family.

5. *Pigs*. Widely regarded as smarter than dogs, pigs are actually quite clean animals. One of the few animals possessing self-awareness, they train easily, and can be fiercely loyal. There have been many recorded cases of pigs saving the lives of their human companions. One chased away an intruder. Another pulled her owner out when she got stuck in a bog. And another even squeezed through a doggie door, ran into the street, and flagged down a car to get

help when her owner had a heart attack. In my book, that's really bringing home the bacon!

6. *Cats*. When it comes to loyalty, felines get a bum rap from dog owners. But that's because they're comparing Abyssinians to Otterhounds. Dogs obey human commands. Cats view them more as suggestions. Cats also don't see their humans as their masters. But that doesn't mean they aren't loyal. They just show it differently. Some common ways are through purring, grooming you, giving you a slow, contented blink, presenting their belly, and giving you a head bunt. (That's not a typo. Cats give head *bunts*, not butts!) Not convinced those cute behaviors count as feline loyalty? Okay, here are some real-life stories that might change your mind:

- When a neighbor's dog attacked a child on his bike, Tara, the family tabby cat, jumped into the fray and chased it away. The whole thing was caught on video and can still be found on YouTube.
- In another story, Schnautzie saved her owner's life when she was still a kitten herself. She woke her owners in the middle of the night and sniffed persistently at them until her humans realized the house had a gas leak.
- Tommy, an orange tabby, managed to call 911 when his wheelchair-bound human fell out of bed and couldn't reach the phone.

Fun Fact: On average, American pet owners spend $1,480 a year on their dogs, and $902 on their cats. This includes food, vet bills, toys, and those must-have treats. Globally, humans spend close to $223 billion on their furry friends each year.

CHAPTER 44
DO THEY COME WITH TEENSY TINY SPIDERS?

Tiny houses are all the rage in the US, with a reported 10,000 of the diminutive homes already constructed by 2019. Some say they're a fad. But according to a report by the Global Tiny Homes Market (yes, it's a real thing) the market for tiny homes is set to grow by $3.57 billion between 2022 and 2026.

Affordability and portability are some of the reasons fueling the tiny house trend. So are financial freedom and environmental responsibility. Check out these tiny home facts:

- The typical tiny house ranges from 100 to 400 square feet.
- Close to 68% of tiny house dwellers own their homes and are mortgage-free.
- Do-it-yourself tiny home builders can construct their abode on the cheap, averaging between $12,000 and $35,000 to complete their projects.

- Tiny houses can be built with solar panels and composting toilets, allowing homeowners to live off the grid.
- Over half of tiny house owners have more savings than the average American.

Sounds good, eh? So what are the drawbacks? Well, if you like your "stuff," you may have a problem. Paring down to the essentials to fit inside a tiny home can require some tough decisions. All those Beanie Babies and grandma's old rocking chair might not be able to make the cut.

If you can get past jettisoning your junk, the next biggest problem is finding a place to park your tiny new home-sweet-home. Many cities and municipalities have a minimum-house-size requirement. Some may label your home an RV if it's permanently mounted on a trailer. Others don't have zoning laws in place, making the places you can park your place up to debate.

In addition, finding room for entertaining people inside a space as big as your bedroom can cut down on your social options. Especially if the weather isn't good enough to barbeque.

One final caveat. According to GNAT (Great Nation of Astonishingly Tiny) Home Owners of America (no, I didn't make that up, either) the divorce rate for couples building tiny homes has doubled (from 25% to 50%) in just three years. Perhaps living alone in a tiny house may be less problematic...

Fun Fact: Tiny, portable houses are nothing new. They date back to at least 1000 BCE, when Mongolia yurts. These round, tent-like houses suited the nomadic lives of the indigenous herders, who were constantly on the move to find new pastures for their livestock. Later cultures developed their own tiny, portable homes, in the forms of wigwams, tents, teepees, and igloos, to name a few.

CHAPTER 45
EXPENSIVE TASTE, INDEED!

GIVEN the way grocery prices have risen lately, I wouldn't blame you for saying chicken wings are the most expensive food on the planet. But they don't even hold a cluck to the priciest potables ever to please a person's palate.

So, what tops the list? (Besides that can of roasted party nuts.) Sink your teeth into these top-ten budget-busting goodies:

1. *Ayam Cemani Chicken*. Originating from Indonesia, these birds are known for their distinctive black feathers and beaks—and the price on their heads. Prized for their tender, flavorful flesh, a single bird can cost $2,000. A restaurant meal will set you back $100 a pound.

2. *Fugu*. No, I'm not trying to insult you. But if you order this puffer fish from the menu, your wallet might take offense. So could your body. You see, fugu is poisonous. It takes three years of training for chefs to learn how to prepare it and be legally allowed to. No wonder it costs around $500 bucks per entrée.

3. *Elvish Honey*. Made from real elves (okay, I made that up) Elvish honey is the rarest in the world. Extracted by cave climbers in Turkey, this honey is prized for its antioxidants and minerals. It's also thought to contain immune-boosting properties, lower cholesterol, and aid in wound healing. But the price itself is quite painful. Coming in at the most expensive honey in the world, Elvish honey costs a sweet $3,091 a pound, or $193 an ounce.

4. *Iberico Ham*. Most people have heard of Parma ham from Italy. Well, Iberico is its even snootier cousin from Spain. Made from the rear leg of black pigs fed exclusively on acorns (bellota in Spanish), the full name of this delicacy is Jamón Iberico de Bellota. Also known as Pata Negra (black paw), it gets its unique flavor from the oleic acid in the acorns it ingests. Hung to dry and mature for 24-36 months, a whole leg can kick your wallet in the teeth to the tune of $4,500.

5. *Bluefin Tuna*. You wouldn't think tuna fish would make the list, but this is no ordinary canned tuna. Much sought after by connoisseurs, Bluefin tuna can cost over $5,000 a pound. In Tokyo, a 600-pound one sold for $1.8 million.

6. *Saffron*. This spice is derived from the flower of a crocus that only blooms once a year. It takes upwards of 75,000 flowers to obtain a pound of it, and the blooms must be harvested by hand. No wonder it's the most expensive spice in the world, coming in at between $5,000 (wholesale) and $10,000 (retail) per pound.

7. *Densuke Black Watermelon*. This rare melon is so sought after in Japan that they can usually only be bought at auctions. A typical winning bid for one is around $6,000.

8. *Wagyu Beef*. Juicier and more tender than ordinary beef, wagyu is known for its intense flavor and tasty fat. Hailing

from Japan, wagyu simply means "cow" in Japanese. The most expensive cuts come from Matsusaka, in Mie Prefecture. In 2002, one of these special virgin, female cows fetched $400,000 at market, so be prepared to bust out some bills if you order wagyu beef.

9. *White Truffles*. And you thought the price of *black* truffles was bad. (LOL). White truffles are even pricier than their cousins, the "black diamonds." Found in the Piedmont and Tuscany regions of Italy, truffles are "sniffed out" of their underground hiding places by trained hogs or dogs. A pound of these *tuber magnatum* will cost you a magnificent $6,000 to $10,000.

10. *Caviar*. No list of luxury foods would be complete without it, right? Caviar is so expensive because it has to be harvested by hand. Today, virtually all sturgeon eggs come from fish farms. Osetra and Beluga caviar are perhaps the two most commonly known kinds. But they're certainly not the priciest. Golden Almus, a caviar from Iran, once held a Guinness World Record as the most expensive caviar, coming in at $34,500. But that record is now held by Strottarga Bianco. This pearl-like white caviar comes from the Siberian Albino Sturgeon. Sprinkled with 22-karat gold, a single teaspoon of the stuff can cost as much as $37,000! I don't know about you, but I find that pretty tough to swallow...

Fun Fact: Kopi Luwak coffee, also known as civet coffee, it's one of the most expensive cups of joe in the world. Why? Because it's made from coffee beans that have been eaten, then expelled by, the Asian palm civet. (A civet is a small, nocturnal mammal that looks something like a cross between an Opossum and a wiener dog.) While the coffee's unusual origins may sound, well, distasteful, it's not just for novelty.

The coffee beans undergo fermentation while they're inside the civet's digestive tract. Drinkers say this results in a smoother, sweeter-flavored brew. Want to give it a try? You can pick up a pound of beans for around $700.

CHAPTER 46
THAT '70'S CEREAL

BACK WHEN I WAS A KID, we picked our cereals based less on the way they tasted than the cool prizes inside that were displayed on the box.

Ever since the 1950s, cereal manufacturers have sought to capitalized on this fact. Throughout the decades, they upped their games, vying for both the pennies in our pockets and our persuasion with our parents. Here are some cool prizes from the 1970s that had us guzzling cereal by the bowlful so we could empty the box, get the prize, and do it all over again. Did you have any of these?

1. *Spy Gadgets*. Spy toys were all the rage in the early 1970s, perhaps due to the Watergate scandal, or the fact that the first James Bond movie, *Live and Let Die*, debuted in 1973. To cash in on the craze, Honey Comb cereal tempted kids with a small, plastic periscope touted as an **Around-A-Corner Viewer**. Not to be out done, Cinnamon Crunch, a Cap'n Crunch spin-off, stuffed a pair of 3-power **Mini Binoculars** in their boxes.

One of the coolest and rarest prizes from 1973 was the

Pink Panther 5-in-1 Spy Kit. It consisted of a telescope, a magnifying glass, and a secret message slot, all disguised as a Pink Panther figurine you could clip onto your shirt pocket. No one would suspect a thing! The reason this is so rare is that the cereal it came in, Pink Panther Flakes, didn't last long past its introduction in 1973.

2. *Glow-in-the-Dark Goodies*. Cap'n Crunch led this section of the pack, offering a glowing acrobats, footprints, **Ghostly Hands**, and **Spooky Pirates**. Specially marked boxes of Super Sugar Crisp offered a glow-in-the-dark pen and various finger-puppet **Monster Heads**, including the Mummy, Frankenstein, Wolfman, and Phantom of the Opera. Boxes of Fruity Pebbles and Cocoa Pebbles offered a glowing **Dinosaur Pen**.

3. *More Monsters.* Apparently, kids loved monsters back then. Besides the glow-in-the-dark ones, Honey Comb offered **Monster Mitts** inside their boxes. The plastic gloves came in ghoulish designs. One was like a scaly sea monster. One had red veins with a spider crawling up the hand. Another appeared as if the skin was unzipping to expose bones. Another had blue veins and an eyeball. **Monster Bike Spin- ners** could be found in boxes of Count Chocula, Franken Berry, and Boo Berry. Made of plastic, they were designed to clip to the handlebars. If you pedaled fast enough, the propeller on them would spin.

4. *Racing Vehicles*. The anticipation always beat the reality of the cool little contraptions shown on the box. In 1975, Freakies Cereal offered one of seven different **Freakmobiles** inside select boxes. By attaching the small plastic bottle supplied to the end of the car and smashing it with your fist, the Freakmobile got a "power boost" and took off. In Post's Pebbles cereals, kids could get their hands on a **Flintmobile**,

a tiny replica of the car Fred Flintstone drove on *The Flint-stones*. It came in four colors and had a removable sun-top.

Other racers included King Vitaman's **Royal Coach** that ran on gyro power. (Winding up a rubber band.) Quisp cereal offered a similar prize shaped like a motorcycle, called the **Gyro Cycle**. Cookie Crisp offered **Mini Skateboards**. Freakies cereal had **Speed Boats**. Peanut Butter Crunch had **Balloon Racers.** Yeah, back then we kids were really going places!

Fun Facts: Besides the awesome prizes above, there were other such odd and memorable toys as: the accordion-like Pebbles cereals' **Flintstone Rock Grabber**, Sugar Bear **3-in-1 Yo-Yo** (it was a whistle, a puzzle, and a yo-yo), the Crunch Berries **Storyscope** (a wristwatch-style magnifying viewer with short adventure stories), Super Sugar Crisp **Action Pinball Games** (they looked like real pinball-machines without the stand), a Sugar Bear **Bike Reflector** (a two-sided reflector shaped like the cereal mascot), and, perhaps the most nerdy prize of all, the Alpha Bits **Pocket Printer**. (It worked by slipping a piece of paper into the plastic device and squeezing. For all that effort, you got a slightly raised letter of the alphabet embossed onto your paper. Riveting, eh?)

CHAPTER 47
A CASTLE FIT FOR A LATVIAN ENIGMA

FLORIDA IS PROBABLY BEST KNOWN for its oranges, alligators, and the tourists who flock there for its beautiful beaches and warm winters. But did you know the Sunshine State is home to one of the most mysterious buildings in the world? To this day, no one has been able to figure out how it was built.

Sometimes referred to as "Florida's Stonehenge," it wasn't built by ancient people in ancient times. Instead, the mono-lithic structure using gigantic blocks of stone was constructed in the 1900s by one lone man from Latvia.

How did he do it? If old accounts are to be believed, he used the same mysterious technology employed by the Egyp-tians to build the pyramids. Is it true? Is it baloney? Read on and decide for yourself.

Coral Castle looks kind of like an old Spanish fort, and is constructed of around a thousand tons of stones shaped into walls, furniture, carvings, and even a two-story castle tower. It can be found lurking near the southern tip of Florida, between the cities of Homestead and Leisure City.

The name Coral Castle isn't the one its builder gave it. The architect of this behemoth, an eccentric Latvian-American named Edward Leedskalnin, simply called it "Ed's Place" when he built it around 1923. His name for it was more accurate, given that the castle isn't made of coral. It's comprised of huge chunks of sedimentary limestone called oolite that can be found just below the topsoil in that area of Florida.

Inside and around the castle grounds, there's a polar telescope, and obelisk, a sundial, a water well, a barbecue, a fountain, and numerous pieces of furniture, including 25 rocking chairs and a table in the shape of Florida. Of course, the king of the castle also needed a bathtub, a bed, and a throne. Astonishingly, with few exceptions, all of these items have been carved from single pieces of stone weighing, on average, around 14 tons each.

The largest stone in the castle weighs 27 tons. The tallest are two monoliths that each stand 25 feet tall. Every stone is held together without mortar. Instead, they're stacked on top of each other in a way that uses their weight to keep them together. The craftsmanship is so precise that no light passes through the joints. The perimeter walls, each made of eight-foot-high vertical stones, still maintain a uniform height, never shifting despite the decades.

Okay, that's pretty impressive, right? But now, consider the fact that Leedskalnin not only built it himself, but that in 1936, he also single-handedly moved the entire thing from Floral City to its current location!

How is the world did he do it? A secretive man, Leedskalnin only worked at night or when nobody else was around. Legend has it he held the secret to reverse magnetism, or possessed supernatural abilities that enabled him to carve the stones and move them around with ease.

He spent over 28 years constructed his castle, refusing to

let anyone witness him at work. A couple of teenagers claimed to have snuck a peek, and reported witnessing Leedskalnin cause blocks of stone to move around like hydrogen balloons. Author Orval Irwin, who reportedly witnessed Leedskalnin quarry stones and erect parts of his wall, illustrated the methods in his book, *Mr. Can't Is Dead.*

The only advanced tool Leedskalnin himself ever spoke about using was a "perpetual motion holder." The website for Coral Castle states, "If anyone ever questioned Ed about how he moved the blocks of coral, Ed would only reply that he understood the laws of weight and leverage well." He also stated that he had "discovered the secrets of the pyramids," referring to the Great Pyramid of Giza.

Leedskalnin continued to work on "Ed's Place" until his death in 1951. He made his living giving tours of the place for a dime a head, then raised it to a quarter. His masterwork lives on today as a privately operated tourist attraction.

Fun Facts: Over the years, Ed's Place continues to attract attention from artists and truth seekers. Here's a sampling:

- In 1944, the Nemith Film Collection produced a short documentary film of Leenskalnin at work.
- In 1958, the film *The Wild Women of Wongo* used Coral Castle as the set for the temple of their dragon god.
- In 1961, lunar scenes in the film *Nude on the Moon* were shot in Coral Castle.
- An episode of *In Search of*, a TV program hosted by Leonard Nimoy, features a dramatization of Leedskalnin moving stones with minimal effort.
- In 1986, Billy Idol's song *Sweet Sixteen* was inspired by the story of Leedskalnin and Coral Castle.

- In 2012, a book released by John Martin entitled, *Coral Castle Construction*, described how Leedskalnin built his structure using fundamental engineering principles.
- In 2014, a segment about Coral Castle appeared on the History Channel's *Ancient Aliens* series. (Season 2, Episode 8: *Mysterious Structures*.)

CHAPTER 48
THERE GOES THE NEIGHBORHOOD

YOU MAY NOT KNOW IT, but we humans are really trashing up the place. Call it space debris, space junk, space trash, space garbage, or space pollution, it's still dumpster fodder.

Exactly how much man-made junk is up there circling over our heads as you read this? At the moment, roughly 129 million pieces, give or take a busted satellite or two.

Most pieces of man-made space debris are pretty tiny. According to the US Department of Defense's global Space Surveillance Network (SSN), as of January 2019, 128 million pieces of debris measuring less than half an inch were swirling around up there. Add to that a further 900,000 pieces measuring under four inches, and that covers the bulk of space junk—as far as numbers go.

But just because a piece of trash is small doesn't mean it can't do any damage. Tiny space debris like flecks of paint and particles of solid rocket exhaust are important enough to space agencies that they grouped them with other micrometeoroids and referred to them as MMODs. (Micrometeoroid and Orbital Debris.)

These "weapons of MMOD" can be quite hazardous to spacecraft, damaging the skin of their hulls like a sandblaster. Solar panels and telescopes are especially susceptible.

For instance, a number of windows on space shuttles have had to be replaced due to damage by paint flecks. In fact, the SSN says these millimeter-sized orbital debris represent the highest "mission-ending risk" to robotic spacecraft that operate in low-Earth orbit.

So what's a poor spacecraft to do?

The International Space Station (ISS) employs Whipple shielding to resist damage from MMODs. Kind of like those soft layers of Charmin bath tissue Mr. Whipple couldn't resist, a Whipple shield uses a multi-layered design to break up impacting objects into smaller pieces. Those getting through the first layer are broken down further by a second layer, then a third layer and so on, until the remaining fragments are too small to penetrate any further.

That takes care of the small stuff. But that still leaves tens of thousands of pieces of dangerous junk orbiting our atmosphere. What's up with them?

The SSN reported it currently tracks more than 27,000 pieces of larger space junk. Around 23,000 of them are bigger than a softball. Others are considerably larger, including abandoned launch vehicle stages, mission-related debris, and even nonfunctional spacecraft.

Considering that, in low Earth orbit, junk and spacecraft both travel around at about 15,700 mph, a collision with even a tiny piece of debris could create huge problems. Recently, several spacecraft, both manned and unmanned, have been damaged or destroyed by space junk.

- In 1996, a French satellite was damaged by space debris from a French rocket that had exploded ten years earlier.
- In 2007, China tested a missile to destroy an old weather satellite, adding 3,500 large pieces to the space junk problem.
- In 2009, a defunct Russian spacecraft collided with a working US commercial craft, adding 2,300 new pieces of large, trackable debris to the list.

How can spacecraft like the ISS avoid all this space trash?

NASA has a long-standing set of guidelines on how to deal with collision threats to the space station. These "flight rules" alert them when tracked debris are expected to be in proximity, and whether evasive action or other precautions are needed to insure the safety of the ship and crew. (In general, if the collision chance with a piece of space debris is over one in 10,000, the ISS is maneuvered to avoid it.)

Fun Fact: Space debris started collecting in October 1957, immediately after the launch of the first artificial satellite, Sputnik 1. We've been junking up the neighborhood ever since.

CHAPTER 49
DO YOU TATTOO?

NOWADAYS, it's hard to go anywhere without running into someone with a tattoo. They can range from exquisitely beautiful to downright pornographic. How did the whole concept of tattooing get started in the first place? And what's spurred its recent resurgence in popularity?

Let's take a look.

The word tattoo was derived from the Tahitian word, *tatau*. It was first introduced to the English language in the late 1700s, when Captain James Cook observed tattooed natives during three voyages to the South Pacific. While in Tahiti aboard the Endeavor, in 1769 Cook made this entry in the ship's log book: "Both sexes paint their Bodys, Tattow, as it is called in their Language. This is done by inlaying the Colour of Black under their skins, in such a manner as to be indelible."

When Cook returned to England, many of his sailors sported tattoos of their own. Cook's science officer and expedition botanist, Sir Joseph Banks, was one of them. However, as a member of English aristocracy, some credit Banks with raising the social status of tattoos. Either way, the men's tattoos reintroduced the artful practice to Europe, and it spread rapidly to seaports around the world.

Of course, the Tahitians weren't the only culture to practice this form of body art. Tattoos can be found in virtually every culture worldwide. For the purposes of this short story, we'll take a look mainly at its history in North America.

The oldest accounts of outsiders encountering tattooed native North American peoples came from Thomas Harriot, a member of the 1585 Grenville Expedition to the Americas. (He was responsible for making observations about the indigenous people encountered.) In *A Brief and True Report of the New Found Land of Virginia*, Harriot wrote about people who had "their skin died and coloured."

The indigenous people of North America have a long history of tattooing. For them, it wasn't done simply to adorn the skin. Instead, each tattoo had deep meaning. Some were used to signal connections to family, places, and societal status. Others highlighted cultural achievements and milestones of maturity. One account from an outsider reported one indigenous people's practice of tattooing the jawline to deaden the nerves that signaled toothaches.

The oldest known tattoo in North America belonged to a mummified Inuit woman found frozen on St. Lawrence Island, Alaska. Radiocarbon dating estimates she lived in the 16th century. Inuit oral traditions tell how the raven and the loon tattooed each other, giving cultural significance to the act. Some Inuit believed a woman couldn't transition into the spirit world without tattoos.

In another example, among the Osage people, men were

often marked with tattoos after accomplishing major feats in battle, as a visual reminder to the community of their bravery and elevated status. As a form of prayer, Osage women were tattooed in public, demonstrating both their strength and their dedication to their nation.

One of the reasons for the rise in popularity of tattoos today stems back to the invention of a device that, while not painless, took much of the agony out of getting one. In 1891, New York City tattoo artist Samuel O'Reilly patented the first electric tattoo machine.

By 1936, one in ten Americans had a tattoo of some form! The majority of people sporting them were sailors, bikers, and gang members, who selected their images from catalogues of pre-made designs known as "flash."

In 1988, a scholar named Arnold Rubin created a collection of works regaling the history of tattoo cultures. Publishing them in *Marks of Civilization*, he also coined the term "Tattoo Renaissance," referencing the technological and social change of the times.

Perhaps Rubin's ideas sparked a movement, or perhaps it was already in motion, but it was around then that wearers of tattoos began to change both the style of tattoos they got, and the reasons behind them. A counterculture of resistance to middle-class values began to show up on their skins. Instead of the same old flash, the new trend was for more customized tattoos. Full-body and full-arm (sleeve) tattoos influenced by Japanese and Polynesian cultures grew in popularity.

By 2012, 23% of American women had tattoos, and 19% of men. In 2013, Miss Kansas, became the first Miss America contestant to display tattoos during the swimsuit competition. Today, some women use the body art as a way to reclaim themselves after abuse or breast cancer. But no matter the rhyme, reason, or design, it appears tattoos are here to stay.

Fun Fact: The oldest tattoo ever discovered on human skin belongs to Ötzi the Iceman. Found frozen in a glacier in the Alps in 1991, Ötzi, who is estimated to have lived around 3250 BCE, sported 61 tattoos.

CHAPTER 50
YOU GONNA FINISH THAT?

BESIDES YOUR COUSIN Tammy gobbling all the deviled eggs at Thanksgiving, competitive eating is a sport usually left to the professionals. After all, you could spring a gut, right?

But did you know that so-called "professional eaters" actual train for the job? Some have learned how to pack away enough food to feed a large family in just minutes! Some go for speed records. Some focus on quantity. Either way, I'm sure they'd have us beat when it comes to chowing down.

Check out these comestible contenders and their world-record skills. I mean, who thinks these things up?

1. *Most Mayonnaise Eaten in Three Minutes*. This gag-worthy record goes to American competitive eater Michelle Lesco. In 2018, she downed 86.35 ounces (about three and half jars worth) in 180 seconds.

2. *Most Chicken Nuggets Eaten in One Minute*. With only 60 seconds on the clock, Leah Shutkever, competitive eater from the UK, downed 19 nuggets in 2022. (She also holds the record for most nuggets consumed in three minutes—1.7 pounds worth!)

3. *Fastest Time to Eat a Jelly Donut with No Hands*. This tasty record went to Philip Joseph Santoro. In 2014, with his hands behind his back, he polished off a jelly donut in 11.41 seconds.

4. *Fastest Time to Eat a Head of Lettuce*. Not quite as tasty as a jelly donut, but a perfect prize for Vegan speed-eater Mike Jack of Canada. In 2021, he wolfed down the whole head in 31.053 seconds.

5. *Most Smarties Eaten in Three Minutes Using Chopsticks*. Throwing a wrench (actually a chopstick) into the works, contestants had to pick up small, pill-shaped candies and get them up into their mouths in order to consume them. In 2013, in just180 seconds, Kathryn Ratcliffe of the UK managed to hoist and eat 175 Smarties—almost one per second.

6. *Fastest Time to Eat Three Carolina Reaper Chilies*. They don't call them "reaper" for nothing. In 2022, American competitive eater Gregory Foster managed to down three of these mouth-scorching peppers in 8.72 seconds. Ouch!

7. *Most Ice Cream Eaten in One Minute*. Now this is one contest I could get into! But I certainly wouldn't win it if Isaac Harding-Davis of Australia was a contender. In 2017, he ate 28.4308 ounces (nearly two containers full) of Ben & Jerry's Strawberry Cheesecake ice cream in a single minute, breaking a Guinness World Record.

8. *Most Marshmallows Eaten in One Minute*. This record goes to Anthony Falzon of Malta. In 2013, he virtually inhaled 25 marshmallows in 60 seconds.

9. *Most Soup Eaten in 30 Seconds*. Known for breaking records guzzling things that don't go down as easy (lemon juice, mustard, ketchup) German competitive eater André

Ortolf broke the record for soup in 2017 by drinking 17.0373 ounces (more than a pound) in half a minute.

10. ***Most Hot Dogs Eaten at Nathan's Famous Fourth of July Hot Dog Eating Contest.*** Perhaps the most famous eating contest of all time, this is *the* prestigious title to hold. Currently, it belongs to competitive eating legend Joey "Jaws" Chestnut. In 2022, he powered his way to his 15th win by downing 63 hot dogs and buns in 10 minutes. (The year before, Chestnut won by downing 76 franks and buns.) I hope somebody gave the guy a TUMS afterward …

Fun Fact: Who holds the record for the most food ever eaten at a single sitting? That honor goes to American competitive eater Bob Shoudt from Royersford, PA. Known as "Humble Bob" or "Notorious B.O.B.," he once downed 23.4 pounds of food in six minutes.

CHAPTER 51
THE REAL BOURNE IDENTITY

IF you ever watched a daytime soap opera, you could bet before the season was out, somebody would be stricken with amnesia. But in real life, instances of unexplainable memory loss are weirder than anything entertainment writers could come up with.

As if ripped from the old adage "Truth is stranger than fiction," one of the more famous cases of amnesia involved a man named Ansel Bourne. (Remember *The Bourne Identity*, the 2002 film starring Matt Damon? It was about an injured assassin who wakes up with awesome killing skills, but no idea who he is.)

Well, something like that *actually happened* to Ansel Bourne. Unlike Damon's character, the real-life Bourne was one of the first documented cases of "dissociative fugue." That's the type of psychogenic amnesia not resulting from injury or disease. It leaves the person able to function normally, but unable to recall their identity.

Anyway, Ansel Bourne was an evangelical preacher from Greene, Rhode Island. On January 17, 1887, he took a trip to visit his sister in Providence. However, unexplainably, he withdrew his life savings and travelled to Norristown, Pennsylvania, instead. There, he opened a variety store under the name of Albert J. Brown and started a whole new life.

Two months later, in the middle of March, Bourne woke up in Pennsylvania with no recollection of where he was or how he got there. He also couldn't remember anything that had happened in the past several months, according to the Historical Society of Pennsylvania. Even more astonishing, in Bourne's mind, it was still January 17. When asked, he had no idea who Albert J. Brown was.

After returning to his home in Rhode Island, Bourne became the subject of study by the Society for Physical Research. Shockingly, under hypnosis, Bourne would assume the persona of Albert J. Brown! Under hypnosis, he relayed a backstory about Brown that was quite similar to his own, but he denied knowing anyone named Ansel Bourne!

After his hypnosis sessions, Ansel Bourne returned to his own persona. He lived out the rest of his live with no further incidents of amnesia, and never assumed the strange, alien persona of Albert J. Brown again.

Fun Fact: Another case of "dissociative fugue" happened to writer Agatha Christie. A world-famous mystery writer, she became the subject of her own whodunit when she suddenly disappeared for 11 days in 1926. When she turned up 200 miles away from her abandoned car, she claimed to have no recollection of where she'd been or what had happened during those "lost" 11 days.

Christie's husband, Archibald, told a newspaper interviewer, "She has suffered from the most complete loss of memory, and I do not think she knows who she is. I am hoping that rest and quiet will restore her." It did.

CHAPTER 52
HOWLING AT THE MOON

BLAMING the moon for our bad behavior is a time-honored tradition. Some say it dates back to the first century AD, when Pliny, a Roman philosopher, suggested that the full moon caused higher levels of dew to form, thus increasing moisture in the brain. This, in turn, he believed, led to madness.

That's my story and I'm sticking to it. Not buying it? Maybe you'll be more inclined to find truth in these recent discoveries about the moon:

In 2009, NASA scientists discovered water on the moon—and it likes to dance around. Water molecules on the moon's surface remain stuck in ice until lunar midday. When it warms up enough to melt the ice, they're set free to float around a bit, before refreezing and settling back to the surface. Other surprising facts include:

- Our moon isn't round—it's oval. The egg shape is due to the Earth's gravitational pull.

- The moon is 400 times smaller than the sun, but is 400 times closer to Earth, so to us humans, they appear the same size, and also allow for a picture-perfect total eclipse of the sun.
- Our moon is shrinking. As its surface crust contracts, it leads to lots of moonquakes.
- On average, the surface crust of the moon is 31 miles thick, and is made mostly of silica, alumina, lime, iron oxide, magnesia, and titanium dioxide, and sodium oxide.
- The moon's diameter is roughly the same distance as from Phoenix, AZ to New York City.
- The far side of the moon, mistakenly called the "dark side," is actually illuminated by the sun just as often as the "bright side" we see from Earth.
- The moon's surface gravity is about a sixth of the Earth's. Its atmosphere, composed of helium, neon, and argon, is ten trillion times thinner than Earth's.
- Scientists still aren't exactly sure how the moon came into being in the first place. They only know that it formed around 4.51 billion years ago, approximately 50 million years after the birth of our solar system.

The moon gravitates around its own axis, showing the Earth only one side of its spherical body—what scientists call the "near side." This illuminated side has a thinner, smoother crust compared to the far side, which is thicker and pocked with impact craters. Why the marked differences? Scientists are still vexed. But the main working theory is that one side was damaged by a massive asteroid impact.

Speaking of which ... researchers detected a gargantuan

blob of metal at the moon's South Pole. It's buried deep below the Aitken basin, the largest preserved impact crater anywhere in the solar system. Weighing in at an estimated 2.4 quadrillion tons, it's believed the ginormous mass is actually altering the moon's gravitational field. Scientists speculate it's the remnants of a massive iron and nickel asteroid that smashed into the moon four billion years ago.

And lastly, perhaps my favorite fact about the moon is this one: Like the beloved Pigpen character in Schultz's *Peanuts* cartoons, the moon is constantly surrounded by a permanent, asymmetrical cloud of dust.

Fun Fact: Temperatures on the moon range daily from negative 279 degrees Fahrenheit at night to 260 degrees Fahrenheit in the afternoon. If you're planning a trip, dress accordingly.

CHAPTER 53
WEINER, WEINER, SPAGHETTI DINNER

IT's a heck of a long way from Piacenza, Italy to Milton, Pennsylvania. But if one Italian man hadn't made the trip, the world would never have fallen in love with Chef Boyardee.

Born Ettore Boiardi in 1897, this American icon is better known by his Anglicized name, Hector Boyardee. Born with ambition in his veins, his culinary training came early. At the age of 11, Hector was already working as an apprentice chef at a restaurant in Piacenza called "La Croce Bianca."

Tired of peeling potatoes and taking out the trash, he decided to follow in his more successful brother Paulo's footsteps. When he was barely 17, Boyardee boarded the French ship, La Lorraine, and headed for the US.

After landing at Ellis Island, Hector got a job with Paulo in the kitchen of the Plaza Hotel in New York City. He worked his way up to head chef, then left for Cleveland to open his own restaurant, Giardino d'Italia in 1924. It was there that he got his idea for Chef Boyardee.

People at his restaurant kept asking him for his spaghetti sauce. Boiardi started selling it to them in repurposed milk bottles. Two regular patrons, Maurice and Eva Weiner, owned a local grocery store chain. In 1927, they helped the Boiardi brothers develop a process for canning the sauce. Smart business people, they also procured US distribution of Boiardi's product through their grocery's wholesale partners.

Soon the brothers' sauce was being stock in markets nationwide. To meet demand, Boiardi moved to Milton, PA and opened his own factory, even growing 20,000 tons a year of his own tomatoes. To help Americans pronounce his name correctly, Boiardi labeled his products Chef "Boy-Ar-Dee."

Besides the original sauce, Chef Boyardee's first ready-to-heat product was a spaghetti kit. Debuting in 1929, the kit contained tomato sauce, uncooked pasta, and a portion of pre-grated cheese. People loved it. His company quickly became the largest importer of Italian Parmesan cheese in the nation.

During WWII, the US military commissioned the company to produce army rations. To keep up production, the factory ran 24 hours a day, with around 5,000 workers churning out 250,000 cans a day.

After the war, Boiardi appeared in numerous print ads and TV commercials touting his brand. He sold the company in 1946 to American Home Foods (AHF) for close to $6 million. He remained a brand consultant and spokesperson for them until 1978. (AHF changed its name to International Home foods in 1996, and in 2000 it was purchased by ConAgra Foods.)

The industrious Italian-American passed away in 1985 at the age of 87, but his legacy lives on. Chef Boyardee canned pasta meals now come in over 30 varieties, from Beefaroni to Chicken Ravioli. But no matter which one you pick, each package still bears the cheerful, smiling likeness of the original Chef Ettore Boiardi.

Fun Fact: On April Fool's Day, 1957, the BBC current affairs program, *Panorama*, ran a story purportedly showing a Swiss family happily harvesting spaghetti from the family "spaghetti tree." (At the time, spaghetti was not widely known in the UK.) Numerous viewers called in, asking advice on growing their own trees. CNN called the broadcast, "the biggest hoax that any reputable news establishment ever pulled."

CHAPTER 54
DON'T BE CAUGHT UNAWARES

TAKE IT FROM ME. There's probably nothing worse than that look you get when you forget your friend's birthday or your spouse's wedding anniversary.

I've been guilty as charged—but it's never intentional. Some of us have a head for numbers and dates, and some of us just don't.

My aunt was the kind of person who bought all her gifts for the entire year during Black Friday and post-holiday sales. I opened her hall closet one day and found her stash. There they were, all beautifully wrapped in birthday paper, graduation paper, baby-shower yellow, and holiday red—a monument to the forgetful, bad-gift-giving loser that I am.

As if surviving the traditional holidays weren't enough, nowadays, every day of the year has become an occasion to celebrate something—no matter how big a stretch. After receiving a calendar marking each one (not exactly a subtle hint) I thought I'd share with you some of the ones I'm looking forward to. Ready? Here goes:

- January 10. National Houseplant Appreciation Day (Uh... too late.)
- January 22. National Polka Dot Day (Except for Czechs.)
- February 12. National Lost Penny Day (Ah, the old Lincoln lean-over.)
- March 1. National Compliment Day (Not bad!)
- March 20. Alien Abduction Day (If only...)
- April 3. World Party Day. (It's about time!)
- April 14. National Moment of Laughter Day (Nice!)
- May 14. World Dance-Like-a-Chicken Day (You sure you really want to see this?)
- May 18. No Dirty Dishes Day. (Yeah, baby!)
- June 22. National Onion Rings Day (Yes, please!)
- July 22. World Hammock Day. (I can hang with that.)
- August 20. World Mosquito Day. (Excuse me, but that's every day in Florida.)
- September 19. International Talk Like a Pirate Day. (Arrgh! I thought I already warned you about this!)
- October 15. Global Handwashing Day. (Uh... shouldn't that be every day, several times a day?)
- October 21. Count Your Buttons Day. (Not exactly blessings, but they are holey!)
- December 8. Pretend to be a Time Traveler Day. (Not hard considering I often feel I must be living on the wrong planet.)
- December 25. A'pahbet Day, or No "L" Day. (A true gift, as no one can email me about their gift, telling me what a 'oser I am!)

Fun Fact: Did you notice there aren't any days mentioned for November? I told you I wasn't good with dates. If you didn't catch it, maybe you should get a calendar, too...

CHAPTER 55
THE LITTLE PIGGY THAT COULD

YOU'VE HEARD plenty of tales of people overcoming adversity, but what about a pig? Get set to meet Chris P. Bacon (yes, that's his real name) and he's the first piglet to ever use a wheelchair!

Born without the use of his hind legs, Chris P.'s chances of even being allowed to live were miniscule. But through luck, love, and pluck, he ended up an international TV star, with three books written about him and well over 118,000 fans following him on Facebook!

The perky, potbellied piglet's story began in Sumterville, Florida, where he was born on a farm. Because of congenital defect, the joints in his back legs were fused, leaving him unable to use them. A woman from the farm took him to a veterinarian to be euthanized. But lucky for the piglet, the vet she chose, Len Lucero, saw something in the struggling animal that made him take a chance on the immobilized pig.

Lucero watched the pig crawl out of the carrier he'd arrived in. "His front legs were down on the ground, his back legs were up in the air, and he was balancing and walking

189

forward," he said. "He was full of life. So I thought, there was no way I could put this thing down. I'd rather give him a fighting chance, at least if not at my home, I would find someplace for him."

Lucero took the pig back to his farm, where his wife and two kids already had a menagerie of animals. Using a set of his son's K'nex toys, he cobbled together a small cart and harness. The pig didn't like it at first, but soon got the hang of the contraption.

A couple of weeks later, Lucero was at a veterinary conference and met a representative from handicappedpets.com. The company, out of Nashua, NH, builds pet wheelchairs, harnesses, and carts. They built a special wheelchair—and a Facebook page—for tiny little Chris P. Bacon.

Lucero videotaped one of Chris P's first jaunts in his new rig, and put it the video on YouTube. Called simply, "Pig in a Wheelchair," it quickly garnered over a million views.

By the time Chris P was six months old, he knew his name, came when called, and was housetrained. He and Lucero also had a three-book deal with Hay House, a publishing company that specializes in self-help and motivational media. Lucero was contracted to write three books about the adventures of Chris, the disabled pig.

Chris P has also appeared on the *Today* show, and met Anderson Cooper. But he most enjoys daily walks with his human family, naps in his plush, air-conditioned pen, and munching on grapes and Cheerios, his favorite foods.

Fun Facts: Today, Chris P has his own webpage, Twitter account, and Pinterest site. He's also been the star of a PBS special about bionic pets. He turned eight on January 13, 2021, and is going strong.

Lucero's books about Chris have inspired thousands of

children with mobility issues. Says Lucero, "I've actually gotten a lot of people on our Facebook site, people with disabilities and people who have gotten recent disabilities. And they say that this little guy ... has inspired them to give it their all. And that give me the tingles in my arms every time I read something like that."

CHAPTER 56
WHOSE IDEA WAS THIS, ANYWAY?

THINK you've done some dumb things in your life? After reading this list of real shenanigans people have pulled, I bet you'll feel like Albert Einstein's smarter cousin:

- A man dressed only in a tutu, broke into a farmer's market and ate fruit and drank a soda. It was all caught on video.
- A man was detained after trying to leave Walmart with $172 worth of steaks and lobsters stuffed in his pants.
- Man wearing a shirt that read, "Who Needs Drugs? No, seriously, I have drugs." was arrested for— drug possession. Who knew?
- When unable to produce a driver's license after being stopped, one man showed the cop his homemade mixed tape of rap music as identification.

- A man was arrested for assault with a deadly weapon after throwing an alligator through a Wendy's drive-thru window.
- In a novel way to pick up a date, one guy drove his girlfriend to a sports bar on a mobility scooter he stole from Walmart.
- A man clad only in his underwear decided to climb up on the roof of a Wendy's restaurant and yell at people. He carried on his public performance for four hours.
- An actual 911 call was placed by a man with a desperate emergency—he was out of vodka.
- A man tired of waiting to be treated in a hospital emergency room decided to steal an ambulance and drive himself home.
- A man was arrested for trying to steal a power pole by strapping it to the top of his SUV. I mean, who would notice?
- A guy robbed a store wearing a bag over his head as a disguise. Only problem was, the bag was transparent.
- A man who tried to "run" to Bermuda inside a plastic bubble had to be rescued by the Coast Guard—*twice*.
- One man denied the accusation that he was drinking while driving, saying he only swigged the bourbon in his vehicle while he was stopped at stop signs.
- A man was arrested for pulling up a chair and eating pancakes—in the middle of a crosswalk.

- One man was arrested for dancing atop a police cruiser. Why did he do it? To escape vampires, of course.

Fun Fact: All of the "events" described above actually happened—in Florida. In fact, so many weird things happen in my state that we have a catchall phrase for less-than-genius behaviors reported by police or caught on camera. These culprits are collectively known as the exploits of "Florida Man."

CHAPTER 57
NACHO AVERAGE TACO

WHO DOESN'T LOVE TACOS? As my favorite food on the planet, I had to dig into some tasty facts about tacos. After all, I'm not the only one who loves them. October 4th is National Taco Day! Hungry for more? Grab some hot sauce and dig in to these savory facts to chew on:

The first tacos could really leave you with an explosive case of ... well, *explosives*. That's because the term "taco" originated in the 18th century from Mexican silver miners. Taco was used to describe the thin sheets of paper that were wrapped around gunpowder to form a crude, early version of dynamite.

The taco as we know it today—a filled tortilla shell—was believed to have been invented between 1000 and 500 BC.

The world's largest flour taco was made in Mexicali, Baja California, Mexico on March 8, 2003. It weighed in at 1.654 pounds.

The longest taco ever constructed was done so in Queretaro, Mexico on November 20, 2011. Filled with *carnitas* (pulled pork), it was 246 feet long and stretched an entire city block.

The most expensive taco in the world can be found at Frida restaurant at the Grand Velas Los Cabos resort in Mexico. Featuring a gold-flaked corn tortilla, langoustines, Kobe beef, Almas Beluga caviar, and black-truffle Brie cheese, this decadent taco will set you back $25,000.

There's a taco etiquette in Mexico. Tradition holds that seafood tacos are meant to be eaten at lunchtime. Little snack-size tacos, called *antojitos*, are meant to be eaten at or after dinner, to stave off nighttime cravings.

The strangest taco filling just might hail from Oaxaca, Mexico. There, locals fill their corn tortillas with *chapulines*— deep-fried grasshoppers! Seasoned with lime and chile, the insects add crunch, along with a yeasty, salty tang some describe as being like wet vinegar potato chips.

Tacos are out of this world—literally! After growing their first successful crop of chile peppers aboard the International Space Station (ISS), a group of NASA astronauts threw them-selves a taco party using seven of the peppers, rehydrated tomatoes and artichokes, and fajita beef. (I wonder if they were less messy in zero gravity.)

Fun Fact: Can't get enough of taco trivia? You're in luck. There's a whole documentary TV series about them! *Taco Chronicles* focuses on the history and culture behind the tasty treats. It premiered on Netflix on July 12, 2019.

CHAPTER 58
KEEP ON TRUCKIN',
BABY!

ARE you a fan of food trucks? Ever thought about setting up one of your own? Either way, here are some interesting tidbits about the culinary crusade cruising across the nation.

Before they sprouted wheels, the first portable food stand was established in Providence, Rhode Island in 1872 by Walter Scott. (No, not *that* Walter Scott.) Seizing on an opportunity to profit from newspaper journalists too busy for a sit-down lunch, Scott cut windows into a covered wagon and placed a sign out advertising pie and coffee for sale. He parked it in front of a local newspaper office and *voila*! The age of fast-food on the go was born!

A couple of decades later, in 1894 similar vendors began showing up at the campuses of Ivy League universities, hawking sausages. But it wasn't until 1936 that someone actually turned a vehicle into a mobile restaurant. Can you guess who?

It was the world-famous Oscar Mayer Weiner Mobile. Shaped like a giant hotdog, it toured the US advertising the company's trademark comestible, often showing up at schools, hospitals, orphanages, and even in parades.

It wasn't until the post-war baby boom of the 1950s that the ice cream truck was born. They, along with other food carts, began appearing outside US Army bases and construction sites, offering busy men a chance to grab a cheap, convenient snack or lunch.

Back then, these portable purveyors of simple, greasy, blue-collar food often earned the dubious moniker of "roach coach," for reasons I'll let you figure out on your own. Still, the new convenience of grabbing a bite on the go persisted, and grew steadily in popularity.

Today, food trucks are all the rage, offering everything from classic burgers to fresh, locally sourced gourmet cuisine. The vehicles they use are truly mobile restaurants, complete with freezers, fridges, ovens, dishwashers, and eCommerce wifi to make it easy to put your lunch on your credit card.

As of 2021, there were over 35,500 food trucks operating in the US, generating an impressive annual revenue of over $1.1 billion dollars.

Ready to start your own? Besides grandma's secret recipes, you're going to need an average of $50,000 for a simple truck with storage and kitchen equipment. Add all the extra bells and whistles, and you could be looking at double that.

So, you've got your truck. You're ready to roll, right? Not quite yet. Depending on which state you plan to set up shop, permits, licenses, and ongoing legal compliance can cost a new food truck owner an average of $28,276 for the first year. Add in employee wages and, all said and done, a start-up food truck business can cost upwards of $125,000. Pretty steep, considering the average annual wage in the food truck industry is $38,064.

As for me, I think I'll stick to being a customer. How about you?

Fun Facts: In 1974, Raul Martinez turned an old ice cream truck into the first taco truck. A smart businessman, he parked it outside a nightclub in East Los Angeles. California has the most food trucks in the US, at 753. Next up is Texas, with 549. Florida comes in third with 502. A typical customer is aged 16-55. Burgers are the most profitable item on the menu.

CHAPTER 59
A LITTLE WEIRD (BUT FRIENDLY) COMPETITION

NOT SURE YOU can grow a giant rutabaga, but you're still itching to explore your inner latent talents? Below are a few light-hearted competitions that take place around the world every year. Who knows? There might be a world-class worm charmer inside you, just waiting to wriggle its way out.

Take a look for yourself at seven of weirdest, funniest-sounding competitions open for almost anyone wanting to participate:

1. *World Worm-Charming Championship*. Where else but England would you find such a silly sport? The idea behind this competition, held each year in Willaston, is to coax as many worms up and out of the ground. How? By creating "good vibrations" in the dirt by rubbing a rod stuck in the ground. Also known as "grunting," participants work their own section of ground. Whoever collects the most worms wins! (Don't worry. Worms gathered are released later that night.)

2. *Totnes Orange Race*. Another utterly English competition, every August crowds gather in the streets of Devon to

watch participants chase oranges down the road. Competitors throw and kick their orange along. The first to pass the finish line is declared the winner. (Legend has it the race was inspired by an incident in the 1500s when explorer Sir Francis Drake knocked over a basket of oranges. The kids ran after them because the fruit was exotic and expensive back then.)

3. *World Gurning Championships*. We're back to England for the ugliest face competition. No, we're not talking about the one you were born with, but the face you can make by twisting up your features. (Also known as *gurning*.) The competition takes place during the annual Egremont Crab Fair. (Established in 1267, it's one of the oldest fairs in the world.) The rules are pretty straightforward. Contestants put their heads through a horse collar and then gurn, baby gurn. May the best ugly face win!

4. *Calaveras County Fair & Jumping Frog Jubilee*. The name might be a mouthful, but that doesn't stop up to 50,000 frog-jumping fans from hopping to Angel's Camp, California each May for this competition. Inspired by Mark Twain's short story, *The Celebrated Jumping Frog of Calaveras County*, frogs are pitted against each other to find out which can leap the farthest. The world record is currently held by Rosie the Ribiter. Owned by Lee Guidici, Rosie jumped an astounding 21 feet, five and three-quarters inches back in 1986. Beat that, and you and your frog could win $5,000 and a gold plaque on the sidewalk called the Frog Hop Hall of Fame.

5. *World Pea-Shooting Contest*. Finally, something you learned in school could actually pay off! Head to Witcham, Cambridgeshire, England in July and claim your spot to prove it. Here, using pea shooters in their mouths, contestants project legumes at a 12-inch-diameter target twelve feet away. Competitors can modify their shooters for accuracy, but must

use peas provided by the contest organizers. The winner gets to bring home the John Tyson Shield. (The contest began in 1971 as a fundraiser by John Tyson, headmaster at a local school. He saw it as a constructive way to harness naughty pupils' penchants for pea shooting.)

6. *US Air-Guitar Championships*. Let that inner rock star shine, baby! Jam with the best air artists at this competition held at various venues every year. The rules are simple: your guitar must be invisible. (Air roadies are allowed, but not backup bands.) The 20th annual event was held in Portland, Oregon in July, 2022. The winner was Rachel "Hott Mess" Sinclair. She brought down the house with her technical merit, stage presence, and awesome wicked "airness."

7. *Mobile Phone Throwing Championships*. Now here's one we can all get behind, right? If you've ever wanted to hurl your phone into a wood chipper, why not go to Savonlinna, Finland and scratch that itch? Held since 2000, contestants throw donated, defunct phones as far as they possibly can. The world record holder is Dries Feremans. He hurled a phone 362.27 feet, earning him an official Guinness World Record.

Fun Fact: The longest moustache in the world belongs to an Indian man named Ram Singh. His Guinness World Record-setting stash measures 18 and a half feet. Ram has been growing it since 1970. He won the title in 2010, and hasn't been beaten since. Ram's secret? He spends around two hours a day "pampering" his moustache, but only washes it every two weeks.

CHAPTER 60
FREE BONUS STORY

Dear Reader,

So, that's it for now! I hope you enjoyed laughing and learning along with me. I know I sure have!

Want to keep the fun going? You can get your copy of Volume 2 on Amazon today!

You can also join my Facebook group and you'll receive a new fun fact on Facebook every Tuesday. Woot woot!

To join, go to Facebook and search for Margaret Lashley – Author.

I hope to see you there soon!

All my best,

Margaret

P.S. Get a FREE bonus story now! Go to: https://dl.book funnel.com/i7y7o1dvnp

P.S.S. Follow me on Amazon and you'll be the first to know when my next book comes out!

See you soon!

Made in the USA
Middletown, DE
13 January 2023

22115358R00106